Michael Adam Beck

AN ECUMENICAL
FIELD GUIDE FOR
FRESH EXPRESSIONS

Abingdon Press™

Nashville

AN ECUMENICAL FIELD GUIDE FOR FRESH EXPRESSIONS

ISBN: 978-1-7910-3390-3
LCCN has been requested.

Menu

Framing

Fresh Expressions is not all that fresh. Consistently across church history, groups of people become fascinated with the way of the apostles articulated in the Scriptures and seek to live that way out in their own time. The unifying theme of this trend could be described as *incarnational mission*—reclaiming the apostolic way of being church from within the rhythms, places, and cultures of the emerging context.

In the ecclesial cycles of stabilization, institutionalization, and professionalization, this activity appears to be a "fresh" or innovative approach.

Thus, Fresh Expressions appears to be a unique movement whose seedlings began to break the surface of the post-Christendom soils of the United Kingdom at the dawning of the twenty-first century. In actuality this movement is connected to a vine of many branches that stretches back across two thousand years of church history.

The word *ecumenical* emerged in the sixteenth century meaning "representing the entire (Christian) world." As an English ecclesiastical word, it was drawn from Latin *oecumenicus*, "general or universal," from Greek *oikoumenikos*, "from the whole world."

In a worldwide historical moment that is defined by increasing polarization, is there a shared purpose that can bring followers of Jesus together in unity? Are terms like *mission* and *evangelism* to be discarded entirely? Or is there a way to repent of the past atrocities committed under those banners and recover the primitive meanings and practices of Jesus and his followers? Is there a way to be a trauma-informed, compassion-centered church? A church that conceives mission as the practice of being good guests, who enter the world of our other in a posture of vulnerability and mutuality. A church where evangelism is an embodied message of wholistic healing for all people and all life. A people who go about mission not only in the *name* of Jesus but in the *way* of Jesus.

Arguably one of the most significant developments of Christianity in the nineteenth century was the Ecumenical Movement. English missionary, Baptist minister, and cultural anthropologist William Carey suggested the convening of an international mission council that would bring together diverse traditions to collaborate around mission in 1810. While several smaller conferences began to meet, it wasn't until 100 years later the first World Missionary Conference gathered in Edinburg, Scotland in 1910. Its significance was in bringing together official representatives from multiple mission societies and denominations to focus on reaching non-Christian peoples. This conference became the forerunner to the modern ecumenical movement—a movement that seeks to take these words of Jesus seriously: "By this everyone will know that you are my disciples, if you have love for one another" (John 13:35).

Might a commitment to reaching new people, in new places, and in new ways again be a unifying force that allows for the celebration of our diverse theological perspectives? As I hope to demonstrate, every Christian tradition that became structuralized as denominations and nondenominations shares values and synergies with Fresh Expressions. For churches to thrive today we need to be adaptive, and this involves anchoring radical change in our core values. This book attempts to help a diversity of church streams discover the Fresh Expressions principles at the heart of our own stories.

In the Fresh Expressions movement every new faith community begins with what we call "double-listening." This refers to tuning our ears to both God *and* context. We immerse ourselves in the community, forming relationships, listening, learning, and loving. Always discovering God is there before we arrive. Rather than bringing God with us or starting new things and asking God to bless our efforts, we begin by discerning what God is doing and join into God's activity.

We prioritize "belonging before believing." Meaning, we create safe communities where we can each be known and loved, regardless of what our religious convictions may or may not be. Believing comes along at the pace of grace for each person, or maybe not at all. We share our faith as a community of equals in the context of these relationships. We do so as we co-create a common language together.

Across two millennia, followers of Jesus have embodied and communicated the essential truths and practices revealed through scripture, refreshing the apostolic ways for new contexts. So, I'll begin by refreshing the material you are reading.

Menu: Rather than a table of "Contents," this book has a "Menu." Contents are *something contained, the subjects or topics covered in a book or document with chapters or other formal divisions of a book or document.* I offer, instead, a menu, which is *a list of options, especially one displayed on a screen, or the food available to be served in a restaurant or at a meal.*

Rather than content to be mastered, fresh expressions are a series of delicious meal options, which you can chose to engage or not. This collection of learnings may provide one idea, one image, one story, which may spark new life in communities and congregations. A meal is a provisional offering; it only stays warm or fresh for a period of time. In a rapidly shifting age, when what tomorrow holds is quite uncertain, we can only share recipes and gather at table one day at a time. I prefer even more for you to think of sitting down together for the most universal Christian phenomenon of all . . . the potluck! Survey the various options and choose to partake of what seems the most mouthwatering.

Movement: There's no "Introduction" here, rather a "Movement." In former days, the church provided foundational narratives—the stories that shaped societies which were part of Christendom. Today, these archetypal stories appear primarily on screens (movie screens, phone screens, and flat screens). Good stories grab you with a movement, a cinematic technique that scans the vista to show what's coming. This movement pans across the fields of Christian history, then and now, serving as the "why" of this book, a vision of what you can expect and an introduction to some key concepts.

Downloads: Rather than chapters, this book has downloads. A chapter is *the main division of a book, typically with a number or title.* Or a chapter can be *the governing body of a religious community, especially a cathedral or a knightly order.* Downloads are a more transparent reflection of what I'm offering. These downloads came through prayer, meditation, engaging scripture, conversation, experience, and research. A download is *the act or process of downloading data.* I downloaded this data from a wide variety of ecumenical church experience, and now I'm curating it as a gift for you to download. You are encouraged to digest it, transform it, and offer it to others for download.

Remix simply means to mix again, or to create a new version by re-combining and re-editing the elements of the existing versions. Approximately midway through each download I will offer a "remix." We will look at the beliefs and practices of various Christian movements, then show how the Spirit is remixing them for the new missional frontier through the Fresh Expressions movement today. Following each download will be a series of "Field Stories."

Field Stories are evidence that followers of Jesus are still taking it to the fields today, through this movement that we call "fresh expressions." I have collected diverse field stories of active fresh expressions practitioners across the globe to demonstrate how the concepts are being lived out today in the new mission reality of the 21st Century.

Missional Field Kits follow the Field Stories as a series of suggested exercises, tools, or discussion questions to try with your team. I envision them as "kits" you can open up and use in your own field.

Credits are the culmination of the work of many beautiful minds. This reference section makes this book more credible.

Alternate Endings are sometimes included in great films. If you read all the way past the credits, there may be something special in store! Can your church experience an alternate ending, rather than the decline and closure so prevalent among churches today?

Movement

Fresh Expressions Across the Fields of History

The first Fresh Expression was cultivated by Jesus of Nazareth sometime around 30 CE. It was a community of the disinherited, living under Roman subjugation. A people seemingly forgotten by the religious systems of their day, "harassed and helpless, like sheep without a shepherd" (Matt 9:36).

In this scenario, Jesus orients his disciples toward the fields, "The harvest is plentiful, but the laborers are few; therefore ask the Lord of the harvest to send out laborers into his harvest'" (Matt 9:37-38).

Jesus's own ministry was not confined to the places considered set apart exclusively for sacred purposes like the Temple or the synagogues. Most of his ministry took place out in the open spaces. The greatest sermon ever preached, the "sermon on the mount," took place on a hillside, not in a sanctuary.

That is not to say Jesus didn't regularly attend the synagogue or visit the temple. However, it's noteworthy that the Gospels don't always describe those moments in a particularly positive manner. Consider the temple tantrum (Matt 21:12-17) and the rejection at the synagogue of Nazareth where they attempted to throw him off a cliff (Luke 4:28-30). Jesus, a faithful Jew, indeed participated in the prevailing religious life of his day. But just like what often repeats across the ages, those at the top of the religious hierarchy rejected and were even hostile toward this fledgling new community.

It is certainly obvious that the spiritual movement that we now call Christianity mostly took place outside the centers of religious and political power. Jesus didn't choose his disciples from among the religious elites or the social influencers. He chose everyday people living ordinary lives. And the church arose in ordinary places.

It was a movement from the fields, and this has been a pattern across Christian history.

Indeed, most great spiritual renewal movements start in the fields. Beginning in the Book of Acts, the faith flourished in new (and disturbing) ways in Antioch. In Antioch, Jewish Christians established a network of house churches, in which gentiles were fully welcomed into table fellowship. Jerusalem recognized the radical nature of this development and called together the first church council (Acts 15). They decided to adapt, celebrate, and support the new emerging faith communities. Perhaps we find ourselves in an Acts 15 moment once again?

Fresh Expressions Across History

Following Acts 15, Luke primarily traces the ministry of Paul. However, consider that Ethiopia is home to one of the oldest continuous churches in the world.

Local tradition identifies the Ethiopian eunuch converted by Philip on the road to Gaza as Qināqis (Acts 8:26-39) and insists that he was martyred for teaching Christianity in Ethiopia (then known as Abyssinia). The *Apocryphal Acts of the Apostles* tell of Mathew making the journey to Ethiopia, working alongside the Ethiopian eunuch, until his execution.

Historians disagree about the validity of these claims, citing a lack of archeological evidence. Yet it is widely accepted that as early as the fourth century, Ethiopia (then known as Axum) had become a Christian empire under King Ezana. Ezana's conversion and declaration of his kingdom as Christian around 347 CE can be validated by royal inscriptions and minted coins.

The fact that the Ethiopian Church represents the formation of the faith in an independent nation, outside the borders of Rome is significant. The Ethiopian church translated portions of the Bible into the ancient Ethiopian language of Ge'ez and to this day balances contextuality (a culturally appropriate form of church) and universality (belonging to the wider church across time and space). This is a church birthed not in Constantinople, Chalcedon, or Canterbury, but rather in Ethiopia. This is an ancient African church, planted not by White European missionaries, but by, with, and for Africans.

The Ethiopian Orthodox Church had a population of at least sixteen million in the early twenty-first century. It belongs to a connection called the Oriental Orthodox Churches. This is a group of six autocephalous (appointing its own head) churches: the Coptic Orthodox Church of Alexandria, the Syriac Orthodox Church of Antioch, the Armenian Apostolic Church, the Malankara Orthodox Syrian Church, the Ethiopian Orthodox Tewahedo Church, and the Eritrean Orthodox Tewahedo Church which together make up 60 million members worldwide.

It was movemental, distributed forms of church, with no buildings and no professional clergy that flourished for 300 years across the Roman Empire. Currently, the earliest building devoted to Christian use is at Dura Europos on the Euphrates River in eastern Roman Syria. It was a remodeled home that came into the possession of Christians in the 240s. The structure had a short life span, as Dura was destroyed by the Sassanian Persians in 256. Emperor Constantine brought a new vision of the church, an amalgamation of church and empire, with the cross as a symbol of holy conquest. Constantine inaugurated an era of grand building projects in the fourth century. He commissioned Christian basilicas to signal his support of the new religion and to advertise his reign.

When Rome began to collapse (476 CE), Christians inhabiting the British Isles were left vulnerable and unsupported in a long period of social and political instability. A Roman once enslaved in Ireland, returned as a missionary sometime in the fifth century. Saint Patrick cultivated a movement of contextual churches beyond the existing centers of church power. Celtic spirituality drew deeply from the Scriptures and the Desert Fathers. It was both a mobile and monastic form of community. Apostolic teams moved about employing the common language and symbols to form incarnational communities among often hostile tribes.

An abbess, Saint Brigid (450–525), founded a missional monastic community there at Kildare and is now revered as one of the three patron saints of Ireland. From Ireland, a missionary named Saint Columba (Colmcille) was sent to the island of Iona in approximately 563 CE. Through his efforts the church took root in Scotland, an incarnational presence among the Pictish tribes. Another missionary monk from Ireland, Saint Aidan, headed to the island of Lindisfarne in 635 CE. Aidan established a similar form of church among the Anglo-Saxon peoples of northern England. These apostles started with listening and learning, then loving and serving the people, building relationships that grew slowly over time as contextual churches sprung up in ordinary life.

Meanwhile, a Roman missionary bishop named Saint Augustine was establishing the church in Canterbury around 597 CE in the southern regions of England. He adapted the Latin tradition to the English people. It was Augustine's church that bore the stamp of Pope Gregory the Great, not Lindisfarne of Iona.

And yet it was Saint Bendict (525) and his order that would become the most resilient form of church for the next millennium. His was an incarnational approach that emphasized the guidance of souls in community. Salvation occurred in relationship with others, and following Jesus included integration of worship, work, study, and service to neighbor. Teams of Benedictines were sent out to start new communities in the under-evangelized places in Europe. This was a spirituality designed for the daily rhythms and places of everyday life.

While the history books often emphasize the activities of these men, groups of women started these kinds of incarnational communities across time and space as well. Consider the semi-monastic movement of lay-women known as the Beguines. This was a group active in Western Europe, in the thirteenth through sixteenth centuries. The Beguines stressed imitation of Jesus's life through voluntary poverty, care of the poor and sick, and religious devotion. They defied cultural and ecclesiastical norms of the time, and were considered fringe, although they cultivated new expressions of church that brought Christian community to everyday life. Their commitment to serving neighbor often included guest houses, medical care, community gardens, and poverty relief.

The Protestant Reformation in sixteenth-century Europe emerged on the edge and posed a challenge to the center of the existing political and ecclesial hierarchy (1517). Martin Luther and other early reformers, such as Huldrych Zwingli, and John Calvin, arose with distinct theologies. These streams of Christian thought were accompanied by contextually formed structures and spread rapidly through the innovation of Gutenberg's printing press. From Protestantism would flow the Puritan Revolution, Spiritualists like George Fox and the Quakers, Pietists like Zinzendorf and the Moravians.

The Roman Catholic Reformation was already underway before Luther's Ninety-Five thesis came along. In Spain, Queen Isabella was committed to Catholic reformation while Luther was still only a boy (1474). A series of edge reforms were attempted by people like Catherine of Siena (1347–1380), Catherine of Genoa (1447–1510), and Girolamo Savonarola (1452–1498), among others. The Fifth Lateran Council (1512–1517) continued earlier attempts at conciliar reform in the same timeframe that Luther took his stand in Wittenburg. New orders were founded, Saint Teresa Ávila (1515–1582) and the Discalced Carmelites who focused on monastic reform, and Ignatius of Loyola and the Society of Jesus (Jesuits) who focused on missional reform. Ignatius wrote the *Spiritual Exercises* when he was a layperson and this movement has profound resonance with fresh expressions.

The English church was deeply influenced by Celtic Christianity. However, since Augustine's archbishopric at Canterbury it had been increasingly aligned with Roman and continental practices. While emerging from a distinct fusion of British, Celtic, and Roman influences, it adopted the episcopal structure of Rome. All that began to change with King Henry VIII in the sixteenth century. The Church of England formally broke with Rome, largely because Pope Clement VII refused to grant Henry an annulment of his marriage to Catherine of Aragon. Henry sought to assume Rome's authority as his own, aligning the power of church and throne.

Upon Henry's death, Archbishop Thomas Cranmer initiated changes that more fully aligned the Church of England with the Reformation. Queen Mary sought to briefly restore Roman Catholicism in England, temporarily thwarted the English Reformation, and ordered Cranmer burned at the stake in 1556. Elizabeth I (1558) assumed the throne and Anglicanism triumphed under her reign for over forty years. The Church of England would come to dominate religious life as a considerable social and spiritual force. Clergy commonly performed the duties of civil servants, and the church's global expansion followed the routes of British exploration and colonization. Anglicanism, for the most part, sought to embody a *via media*, a middle way between Catholicism and Protestantism.

However, the church's hold on English religious life began to wane in the eighteenth century. The Anglican Church began largely failing to reach many common people. There was a growing gulf between the wealthy minority and the immobilized masses experiencing poverty. It was a time of enormous social and economic change and dislocation which included massive population growth as well as urbanization. The Industrial Revolution was dawning, and the seeds of a global economy were being planted. There was a sense that the episcopal bureaucracy had become rigid, unyielding, and lifeless.

The Evangelical Revival arose in response—a movement from the *fields*. While it had many points in common with earlier Low Church attitudes and with sixteenth and seventeenth century Puritanism, it emerged as a distinct form of incarnational mission. George Whitfield, John Wesley, Charles Wesley, and others joined what the Holy Spirit was up to outside formal ecclesial spaces with people who largely had no relationship with the church. The awakening was formed from a passion to connect with people outside the reach of the current structure of the church, igniting several missional innovations. This movement would soon reach across the pond to the newly forming colonies.[1]

Fresh Expressions in the Americas

While the emergence of the church in North America is often traced by protestants through Eurotribal settlers, the Oldest Native American congregation, and one of the oldest congregations in the United States (1598), is San Juan Bautista Church in Ohkay Owingeh (formerly San Juan Pueblo), New Mexico. The first churches were established by the Roman Catholics. The Cathedral Basilica of St. Augustine is the oldest parish in continuous existence in the United States of America. The parish was established September 8, 1565, as San Agustin de La Florida, by Spanish conqueror Don Pedro Menendez de Aviles.

It must be noted that the land on which the church took root in North America is stolen. Many Christian traditions overlook an entire history of indigenous people. Various tribes migrated to the continent and occupied these lands for at least 20,000 years. Hence, Europeans arrived in what was to them a "New World" but for the indigenous population, this was the land they called simply *home*. These native inhabitants are people of sophisticated and mature cultures, and religions. They share a rich tapestry of established languages and history.

---

1. Justo L. González, *The Story of Christianity. Volume 1: The Early Church to the Reformation*. Rev. and Updated [ed.], 2nd ed. New York: HarperCollins, 2010.

For North Americans, the deepest level of our soil is soaked with blood. The first settlers of these lands were not White, and the takeover of land was done in a way not reflective of our Christian teachings. The treatment of indigenous peoples is a sad and dark legacy of our nation, and one that is important to acknowledge and make amends for. Reparation must include to some degree the return of stolen land. Today, six in ten Native Americans (60 percent) identify as Christian. Additionally, the Native American Church alone, a syncretic Native American religion that teaches a combination of traditional Native American beliefs and elements of Christianity, has 250,000 members.

Alongside the mission activities of Catholics, the movement that began in the fields of England swept across the Atlantic Ocean and took root in a fledgling United States and Cananda. Protestant circuit riders crisscrossed what was for them a new frontier, planting churches across the massive landscape. They left in their wake a constellation of new Christian communities, many of those located in rural areas outside urban centers. These ministers were unified in a commitment to form new Christian communities in the most remote places of the far-flung terrain.

Reports from across the field in the spring of 1802 described a religious awakening that was "spreading along like a moving fire."[2] This sweeping revival led Presbyterian minister Charles Finney to refer to Western New York State, an area particularly active with emerging insurgent groups, as the "burnt district."[3] Meaning, the region was so set ablaze with spiritual fervor it was left smoldering.

The congregations founded in this period became the centerpiece of USAmerican life for a time. The place where people gathered not only on Sundays to hear a sermon, but to help each other work the land, break bread, and form deep relationships. The church was the place where they found a community that could sustain them through the joys and

2.   John H. Wigger, *American Saint: Francis Asbury and the Methodists* (Oxford New York: Oxford University Press, 2009), 315.

3.   Charles Grandison Finney, *Autobiography of Charles G Finney* (1876).

struggles of life with the land. Churches became the guiding hand in the life of these places.

Jeffrey Williams, professor and researcher on religion and national identity in the Early American Republic notes there has been some debate as to what level these insurgent Christian movements shaped the "American Mind." Did these Christian trailblazers provide the content, inspiration, and structures for colonists to imagine a new political entity birthed through revolution? Revivalism, at least indirectly, fueled the Revolution by establishing structures and new patterns of leadership, communication, and public participation that bred and sustained resistance to traditional authority.[4]

In the wake of the Revolution, individualism, dissent, and democracy, became ideals that were taken up into a new iteration of American Christianity. A group of insurgent leaders, Baptist, Christian, Universalist, Disciple, Millerite, Methodist, and Mormon arose and sought to catalyze a movement of new forms of church among ordinary people. Nathan Hatch notes of these leaders, "They shared an ethic of unrelenting toil, a passion for expansion, a hostility to orthodox belief and style, a zeal for religious reconstruction, and a systematic plan to realize their ideals" and perhaps most notable . . . "they all offered common people, especially the poor, compelling visions of individual self-respect and collective self-confidence." Each of these emergent leaders was also highly skilled in communication and group mobilization.[5]

A common theme among these groups and their leaders is an impulse towards democratization, of which Hatch writes, "has less to do with the specifics of polity and governance and more with the incarnation of the church into popular culture." He lists, three key ways these movements articulated a democratic spirit:

---

4. Jeffrey Williams, *Religion and Violence in Early American Methodism: Taking the Kingdom by Force* (Bloomington, Ind: Indiana University Press, 2010), 60.

5. Nathan O. Hatch, *The Democratization of American Christianity* (New Haven, CT: Yale University Press, 1991), 18.

First, they denied the clergy laity distinction.

Second, they empowered ordinary people.

Third, they held an audacious belief that authoritarian structures would be overthrown.[6]

American Christianity was a barnstorm in the backcountry. A host of emerging popular leaders stepped forward into the fields with a democratized Christianity: Henry Alline, Alexander Campbell, John Leland, Barton Stone, William Miller, Lorenzo Dow, Peter Cartwright, Joseph Smith, and more. Waves of women, and persons of color, took leadership of the movement in new and revolutionary ways. Harry Hosier, Richard Allen, Barbara Heck, Ellen Gould White, Jarnea Lee, Sojourner Truth, Phoebe Palmer, and many others, began laying the foundation for women's rights, temperance, and abolition.

Early Presbyterian settlers were among the first reformed denominations that planted churches across the colonies and dominated American colonial life at the time of the Revolutionary War. Their rejection of both episcopal and congregational polity, in favor of a form of church governed by representative assemblies of elders, would be mirrored by an American Republic which rejected both a monarchy and a pure democracy. Presbyterians helped create state and national constitutions and the structure of American government itself.

While these developments are the feature story of most history books, an "invisible church" was also developing amid the horrors of the Atlantic Slave Trade among enslaved Africans. The late Dr. Janet Duitsman Cornelius notes in *Slave Missions and the Black Church in the Antebellum South* that while many enslaved people gathered publicly for worship organized by White missionaries, they also gathered secretly in Hush Harbors. This was its own kind of mixed ecology of church.

---

6. Hatch, *Democratization*, 25–26.

Hush harbors were meeting places created by enslaved persons outside the plantation quarters for a more incarnational form of church that integrated the African worldview. They created sacred space, often secretly, amid rivers, hills, forests, swamps, and coastlines. Typically, these were wooded and secluded spaces. The term *hush harbor* has parallels with *brush arbor* or *brush harbor*, the names that Whites gave to the open-air campmeetings they convened in groves and fields along the frontier.[7]

Campmeetings radically democratized social relationships. People once excluded from public authority, persons of color, women, slaves, and the unlearned, now claimed leadership alongside those with positions of power. The gatherings were often ecumenical, unifying protestant denominations. All sorts of insurgent groups were present, worshiping together, with a collective vision, and missional purpose.[8]

Campmeetings openly defied ecclesiastical standards of time, space, authority and liturgical form. Campmeetings moved beyond field preaching, shifting attention from conspicuous preaching performances to congregational participation. Supernatural manifestations, and uncensored testimonials by persons with no respect to age, gender, or race were normative. Public sharing of private ecstasy, overt physical display and emotional release, loud and spontaneous response to preaching, and the use of folk music were included among innovations.[9]

African Americans, both free and slaves, were attracted to the informal and spontaneous nature of these gatherings. They participated as equals alongside Whites. The message of personal holiness cut across racial, social, and economic lines, and Blacks were encouraged to become preachers.[10] Harry Hosier, the legendary Methodist preacher, was one who responded to the call. While for a time campmeetings created a sense of liminality in

---

7.   Janet Duitsman Cornelius, *Slave Missions and the Black Church in the Antebellum South*. (Columbia: University of South Carolina Press, 1999), 18.

8.   Williams, *Religion and Violence in Early American Methodism* 111.

9.   Hatch, *Democratization*, 77.

10.   Webb, Stephen, 34.

which the expected social hierarchy was challenged and reimagined, sadly, as these movements began the process of institutionalization they reverted to racist tendencies and segregation.

While the campmeetings were a positive movement toward racial harmony and social equality for a time, the hush harbors were a space where African lore, cultural wisdom, and practices could be experienced and preserved. The secret sites were constructed with poles, brush, and rough planks. Small logs served as seats. Large pots were turned upside down and used for noise control. These hush harbor locations even became the first sites for Black churches after emancipation. Most of the first Black churches which were formed before 1800 were founded by freed Black people. Today 75 percent of Black American adults identify as Christian, many of whom trace their spiritual ancestry through this line.

In Canada, French colonization began in the seventeenth century with Roman Catholics establishing a francophone population in New France, which is now mainly Nova Scotia, New Brunswick, and Quebec. Waves of Anglicans and other Protestants brought British colonization to Upper Canada, now Ontario. The Russian Empire spread Orthodox Christianity in a small extent to the tribes in the far north and western coasts.

In South America, many early conquistadors sadly employed a "replacement model" of mission. This involved going into foreign territory and literally attempting to wipe out the people who were already there. Later, the "ennoblement model" of mission took root, in which natives inhabiting the land were viewed as primitive, non-enlightened cultures, and if they were Christianized, they would become enlightened like the supposedly superior Eurotribal peoples. Unfortunately, this is more tragic history and reparations are yet to be made.

For centuries Roman Catholicism was the dominant Christian influence on indigenous peoples in South America. In the 20th century various forms of Protestant Christianity began to flourish, especially Evangelical and Pentecostal. And yet, indigenous forms of church have flourished alongside those inherited expressions. According to Pew Research Center

83.43% of the South American population is Christian, although less than half of them are considered "devout."

In recent decades, the Base Ecclesial Communities movement has arisen and been reflected upon by liberation theologians of Latin America like Leonard Boff. Boff is a Franciscan priest who describes the "base ecclesial communities" of Brazil in his book *Ecclesiogenesis: The Base Communities Reinvent the Church*. Boff employs the language of the basic community (as described in the seminar held in Maringá, Brazil, from May 1 to 3, 1972, which examined these communities) as "a group, or complex of groups, of persons in which a primary, personal relationship of brotherly and sisterly communion obtains, and which lives the totality of the life of the church, as expressed in service, celebration, and evangelization."[11]

Boff posits that the particular church is the universal church rendered visible within the framework of a time and a place, a medium and a culture. Meaning, each of these particular church communities are sacramental, a means of God's embodied grace in the world. Being that the basic church communities represent, in part, the "true, universal church" they can revolutionize the church by turning the focus from structure to community. Boff argues that basic church communities help shift the hierarchical structure of the church from "steeple down" to "foundation up" by giving laity a greater level of shared power in the church.[12]

Boff argues that base communities are not just another movement within the church, but rather these are churches in themselves, among the people, in the church's foundations. He writes, "The basic communities are a response to the question: How may the community's experience of the apostolic faith be embodied and structured in the conditions of a

---

11.   Leonardo Boff, *Ecclesiogenesis: The Base Communities Reinvent the Church* (Maryknoll, NY: Orbis Books, 1986), 25.

12.   Boff, *Ecclesiogenesis*, 25.

people who, in Brazil as throughout Latin America, are both religious and oppressed?"[13]

The base communities recover the subversive nature of the church. They connect people into what sociologist Manuel Castells calls "resistance identity" which is generated by actors who are in devalued conditions within the dominant structures but who embody values opposed to those permeating the institutions of society. The identity of resistance leads to the formation of communes or communities, which is collective resistance against oppression or the dominant culture defined by history, geography, or biology.[14]

These small faith communities of resistance help people connect and organize at a grass roots level. It's easy to see how these communities reintegrate church planting and social justice. Base communities have many parallels with fresh expressions. They bring the communitarian elements into coexistence with the institutional elements, which can lead to wholistic renewal. This has been a repeated pattern across the history of the church.[15]

Indeed, as long as the Christian faith has existed, there have been movements that bare the marks of what we call today . . . Fresh Expressions of Church. Perhaps across the span of our Christian traditions we can find common ground and unity in our mission. Across the ecumenical spectrum, we may forge new allyships in our commitment to see a movement of new Christian communities spring up in the fields. We might recover the fresh expressions elements at the core of the story of our own traditions.

Time for a Remix

Once again, the Spirit is up to something out in the fields with the "nones" (people who claim no religious affiliation or practice) and "dones"

13.   Boff, *Ecclesiogenesis*, 25.

14.   Manuel Castells, *The Power of Identity*, 2nd ed., vol. 2 of *The Information Age: Economy, Society, and Culture* (Malden, MA: Wiley-Blackwell, 2010), 8–9.

15.   Justo L. González, *The Story of Christianity. Volume 2: The Reformation to the Present Day*. Rev. and Updated [ed.], 2nd ed. New York: HarperCollins, 2010.

(people who once practiced a religion, but no longer do) of our post-everything society. Fresh Expressions is an ecumenical movement with churches across the theological spectrum. So, this book is a practical "field guide," live from the fields where a new kind of church is springing up from the ground.

Are you ready for déjà vu? Once again, the structures of society are engaged in massive transformation. Once again, much of the inherited church is not connecting with the larger population or engaging the culture in transformative ways. So an informal ecumenical group led primarily by Anglicans in the UK organized to create a report concerned with the continued decline of the church and the emergence of new ecclesial communities.

The preface to the Declaration of Assent that all incoming Anglican clergy must confess says,

> The Church of England is part of the One, Holy, Catholic and Apostolic Church, worshipping the one true God, Father, Son and Holy Spirit. It professes the faith uniquely revealed in the Holy Scriptures and set forth in the catholic creeds, *which faith the Church is called upon to proclaim afresh in each generation.* (italics mine)[16]

The phrase "Fresh Expressions" emerged from the conviction in this statement, with the team led by Bishop Graham Cray, who produced the *Mission-Shaped Church* (MSC) in 2004. The report became an international bestseller, is credited with transforming the ecclesiology of the Church of England, has catalyzed the development of thousands of fresh expressions, and released similar initiatives in Australia, Canada, mainland Europe, South Africa, the United States, and elsewhere.[17]

---

16. Graham Cray, *Mission-Shaped Church: Church Planting and Fresh Expressions in a Changing Context* (New York: Seabury, 2010), 100.

17. Michael Moynagh, *Church in Life: Emergence, Ecclesiology and Entrepreneurship* (London, UK: SCM Press, 2017), 2.

A fresh expression is a form of church for our changing culture, established primarily for the benefit of those who are not yet part of any church. These are forms of church that are

Missional: birthed by the Spirit to reach not-yet-Christians.

Contextual: seek to serve the context in an appropriate form to the people in it.

Formational: focused on making disciples.

Ecclesial: a full expression of the "church" not a stepping-stone to an inherited congregation.

The *Mission-Shaped Church* showed incredible insight to recognize the massive shift in the structure of society and the need for new forms of church. As Cray put it, "The Western world, at the start of the third millennium, is best described as a 'network society.' This is a fundamental change, 'the emergence of a new social order.'"[18]

Pioneering sociologist Manuel Castells posits that at the end of the second millennium, a new form of society arose from the interactions of several major social, technological, economic, and cultural transformations: the network society. We are currently now in a period of historical transition between different forms of society, moving from the Industrial Age into the Information Age. The network society consists of a social structure made up of networks enabled by microelectronics-based information and communications technologies.[19]

In sociology, field theory refers to the environments in which interaction between individuals and groups take place. We often think of fields in terms of markets, academic disciplines, musical genres, etc. But fields simply refer to the social space and various positions that social actors can occupy.

---

18. Cray, *Mission-Shaped Church*, 4.

19. Manuel Castells, *The Rise of the Network Society* (Oxford and Malden, MA: Blackwell, 2000), xvii–xviii.

The "fields" referenced earlier from which movements often occur have changed. Consider an examination of the "space of flows" and the "space of places" in a network society (*flows* are the means through which people, objects, and information are moved through social space). Multiple layers of networks, digital and physical, intertwine, connecting people in nodes and hubs, which we will explore as the first, second, and third places of local communities. These are the new "fields" of the Information Age.

Fresh Expressions are a powerfully effective way to engage this emerging societal milieu. The *Mission-Shaped Church* team didn't initiate the fresh expressions movement. They observed how the Holy Spirit was reaching non-Christians and forming disciples of Jesus Christ where they already shared life. They provided language and began seeking to understand the movemental process of something God was initiating. By realizing the Holy Spirit was once again up to something out in the fields, the *Mission-Shaped Church* helped birth a cross-denominational movement, tethered to and alongside the institutional church.

Alan Hirsch and Dave Ferguson note that every historical renewal movement, recovers some degree of the following movemental elements: priesthood of believers, "kingdom of God" over "church," prophetic protest, church planting, mission on the fringes and among the poor.[20] It seems that these missional waves of the Spirit are always breaking on the shore of history.

The Fresh Expressions movement is emerging before our eyes in real time. Increasingly more Christian traditions are paying attention to what the Holy Spirit is up to. Now we have new processes, language, and resources to join in. Entire conferences, denominations, dioceses, networks, and beyond are catching on, embracing the movement, and entering into partnerships. We are catching this wave of the Spirit together!

---

20. Alan Hirsch and Dave Ferguson, *On the Verge: A Journey into the Apostolic Future of the Church* (Grand Rapids, MI: Zondervan, 2011), 35.

I am a Methodist. More specifically I am a continuing United Methodist. I know this self-description will elicit different images and stereotypes from many readers, many which are not positive. Let me explain what that means to me. I am writing as someone who has been nurtured, formed, educated, and supported by a denomination that loved me into being. This love reaches back to my experience as an abandoned child in my infant baptism. A United Methodist congregation became my orphanage, they committed to raise me in a community of love and forgiveness.

I am also someone who sees deep flaws in the denomination that I love. It seems I have become an equal opportunity offender. I draw critique from both sides of the theological and political polarization that marks our age. But I have chosen to be a person who reforms from within, and as a Wesleyan, this is an essential trait of our movement.

I've written this book for people who love their tradition, want to steward it well, and see the need for deep reform and renewal. I see Fresh Expressions as a pathway to bring forth the best of our core stories for the renewal of our traditions. While I can't lay aside my Methodist-ness, what I am attempting to do is show how this is a movement for all of us.

I serve as the Director of Fresh Expressions for The United Methodist Church. I was the first clergy person appointed to this new role in the United States. Florida was the first conference to launch a formal fresh expressions initiative under the leadership of Bishop Ken Carter. I live in a state where most congregations are in decline, less than 18 percent of the population is in worship on the weekend, and churches across the denominational spectrum close their doors every week. We have a goal of five hundred fresh expressions of church by 2025. Now, amid the tsunami of closures and disaffiliations, over three hundred fresh expressions of church have emerged.

God's way of making "all things new" is not the same as our infatuation with brand newness. God takes the existing material and reworks it. Like a potter at the wheel, God takes what's marred and makes something new. God takes fragmented lives and reworks them into a mosaic of grace.

Resurrection is about taking what's dead and decaying, and through a marvelous work of renewal making it eternally alive again. God is in the process of making the entire cosmos new in this way (Rom 8:18-23).

H. Richard Niebuhr once said, "The great Christian revolutions come not by the discovery of something that was not known before. They happen when someone takes radically something that was already there."

There is no "golden age" to which we should return. Before us now is an adaptive challenge. No amount of applying technical solutions to technical problems will reverse the decline.[21]

The fresh expressions movement is not the next newfangled thing. This is a movement of the Holy Spirit, a new iteration of Christians taking it to the fields again. It enables us to be church with people who will never come to our Sunday morning services and yet continue to serve the people who will. It is an awakening of the core identity of who we are as followers of Jesus. It is not in competition with our traditional activities as a congregation—it is a complement.

Furthermore, it's not only for large churches with staff and resources. I am serving as a co-pastor and co-planter of a network of revitalization congregations that had dwindled down to a handful of people. My wife and I currently share responsibility for two inherited congregations (Wildwood and St Marks, Ocala), a new church plant (Compassion UMC), and a network of a dozen fresh expressions meeting in every nook and cranny of life. I am not a theorist. I'm imperfectly seeking to live out every day what I write about here. I am reporting live from the fields, not from the confines of the study.

Our churches are now considered models of the "mixed economy" or "blended ecology way." The *mixed economy* refers to a diversity of ecclesial forms in which fresh expressions of church exist alongside inherited forms in relationships of mutual respect and support.[22] The *blended ecology* refers

---

21. Kenneth Carter and Michael Beck, *Gardens in the Desert* (Nashville: Abingdon, 2024).

22. Michael Moynagh, *Being Church, Doing Life: Creating Gospel Communities Where Life Happens* (Grand Rapids, MI: Monarch, 2014), 432.

to fresh expressions of church in symbiotic relationship with inherited forms of church in such a way that the combining of these modes over time merge to create a nascent form.[23]

While the purpose of fresh expressions is to reach non-Christians and be church with them where they are, churches that plant fresh expressions are experiencing renewal. Through fresh expressions not only are people being offered Christ for the first time, but inherited congregations are being revitalized by this approach. Joining into the movementum of fresh expressions allows existing churches to catch a fresh breath of resurrection. Our own inherited congregations have experienced forms of revitalization through cultivating fresh expressions in our communities.

While some claim mainline denominations traded our missional zeal for respectability, the Fresh Expressions movement is allowing us to reclaim our core and vital DNA. Institution and movement are beginning to operate together in a life-giving way. Can we learn to do so without once again exiling the very apostolic impulses that may give us life? Can we learn from our past mistakes to make possible a new future? Can we embrace both a neighborhood and a network approach to mission? Can we realign our systems to make room for incarnational ministry?

---

23. Michael Beck, *Deep Roots, Wild Branches: Revitalizing the Church in the Blended Ecology* (Franklin, TN: Seedbed, 2019).

Jesus Is Lord of Neighborhoods and Networks

Many Christian traditions understand themselves as a revival of primitive Christianity. They often perceived a discontinuity between the church of their day and the early church. Central to the activity of incarnational mission is returning to the first principles of scripture, which can require significant adaptation. Studying "renewal movements" within the larger church there are key themes like rediscovery of the Bible, recovering a priesthood of all believers, and an awakening of the theology of the first apostles. Let's begin this journey by pondering the central claim of the early church, "Jesus is Lord" and how it's awakened in the fields.

The first Christians gathered around the confession of Jesus's Lordship, a title they believed was conferred on Jesus by God, based on the resurrection (Acts 2:32-36). After they saw Jesus resurrected bodily, they experienced him from then on, through the power of the Holy Spirit, as infinitely alive on both personal and communal levels (1 Cor 12:3). The Lordship of Jesus is a central theme of the New Testament, from the prenatal confession in the womb of Mary (Luke 1:48) to the final benediction of John of Patmos in Revelation (Rev 22:20-21).

The early church's designation of Jesus as χύριος (*kyrios*)—Lord— was politically subversive in an empire where Caesar was declared Lord. Furthermore, the disciples worshipped Jesus as God, and this belief was passed down and articulated formally in 325 CE in the Nicene Creed, which clarifies Christ is "of one substance with the Father, begotten, not created."[1]

This personal relationship with the living Jesus, and allegiance to his Lordship was something that marked missional movements across history. The Lordship of Christ is a basic Christian doctrine. However, consider that for Baptists, this has a special meaning in the tradition that informs other key Baptist beliefs, such as those about the authority of the Bible, soul competency (the accountability of each person to God), religious freedom and the nature of the church that is modeled after the New Testament.

For Baptists in the 1600's this caused tension and even martyrdom. Baptists interpreted Lordship to mean that persons and churches ought to be free from coercion by government or religious organizations in spiritual and religious matters. This put Baptists at odds with King James I, who claimed to be the head of the Church of England as well as of the government of England. The king expected churches to submit to his will. Thomas Helwys, an English minister, was one of the joint founders, with John Smyth, of the General Baptist denomination. Helwys wrote a book entitled *A Short Declaration of the Mystery of Iniquity* in which he insisted that the king had no right to dictate to persons and churches what to believe. King James imprisoned Helwys where he languished and died.

Later, a central aspect of the Evangelical Revival involved a recovery of the Lordship of Jesus, which included stories of personal experience and conversion. These stories were shared through the emerging print media of the day, helping to advance the movement. It was something seemingly

---

1. Henry S. Bettenson and Chris Maunder, *Documents of the Christian Church* (Oxford: Oxford University Press, 1999), 27.

absent in the institutional forms of the church and the clergy, whom John Wesley frequently described as being Christians in name only.[2]

Historically, we have tried to grasp what this Lordship means by understanding it in "spheres." In the *personal sphere*, Jesus is Lord of the individual Christian. To say that Jesus is Lord means we put our whole faith and trust in him, surrender to his authority, and agree to let him be the ruler of our lives, one day at a time. In the *communal sphere*, Jesus is Lord of this community called the church—including local churches, denominations, and the universal church (Eph 5:23; Col 1:18).

That brings us to the *social sphere*—Jesus's Lordship is not limited to the church but encompasses all societies. All human claims to power are subject to Jesus. This assertion may seem at first glance like a conundrum in a world plagued with terrorist attacks, inequality, racism, poverty, and corruption at every level of most governments. One might ask, "How can Jesus be Lord of this?" One role of the church is to work among these fallen societies of the earth to bring the realization of Jesus's Lordship to bear. Indeed, Jesus and his followers have undeniably reshaped the societal sphere in incalculable ways for two thousand years.

This transformation has been a focus of many Christian traditions.. It includes a commitment to both *personal holiness* and *social holiness*. We participate in works of piety that help us grow in love for God: prayer, studying scripture, worship, fasting, Holy Communion, and so on. We also expect our faith must be expressed in our works of mercy, that is, actions that seek justice and reconciliation for all people. In these ways, we seek to grow in love for our neighbor. Yet, we also realize that Jesus's reign has both future and present dimensions (Matt 13:33). From kings and queens, local mayors, to presidents, and dictators, every human claim to power is hollow and ultimately accountable to Jesus (John 19:11; Phil 2:10-11). In the *cosmic sphere*, Jesus is Lord of the entire universe (Col 1:15-17).

---

2. Ryan N. Danker, *Wesley and the Anglicans: Political Division in Early Evangelicalism* (Downers Grove, IL: IVP Academic, 2016), 89.

Consider that John Wesley is sometimes called a "folk theologian" who cobbled together the essential theological emphases of Continental Pietism and Eastern Orthodoxy into a "practical divinity." The previous (seventeenth) century saw regicide, socio-cultural upheaval, and the bloodshed of the English Civil War in which Christians killed each other in the name of the Prince of Peace. This was a scar on the living memory of the people, who in Wesley's day were in a time of national restoration. The age of the Industrial Revolution was dawning. Anything that threatened the *Pax Anglica* was highly suspect. The larger Evangelical Revival that Wesley influenced was a threat. There was in general an underlying deep skepticism of the church, and the activities of the first Methodists seemed to threaten what little emerging stability there was.

Wesley was significantly criticized by those who viewed the parish system as sufficient for reclaiming lost souls and making Christian converts in its current state. In defense of field preaching, Wesley wrote, "Therefore, it is evident that there are not churches enough. And one plain reason why, notwithstanding all these churches, they are no nearer being reclaimed, is this—they never come into a church, perhaps not once in a twelve-month, perhaps not for many years together."[3] From Wesley's perspective, people were not coming "into a church" and the current parish system was insufficient for reaching the majority of people.

Furthermore, the Age of Enlightenment was creating a false dichotomy between faith and reason and moving society "forward" toward the latter in the name of progress. The emphasis of reason and scientific certainty penetrated the church and created a culture of detached Deism. A new protest from reason pushed against the Christian faith itself, and the first cracks resembling post-Christendom emerged. Wesley felt many clergy had abandoned the orthodox faith for enlightenment ideals.

Meanwhile, crime, alcoholism, and poverty plagued the general populace. Soldiers returning from the war between England and France joined

---

3. John Wesley, et al., *The Works of John Wesley* (Nashville: Abingdon Press, 1984), Vol. VIII p. 113. *A Farther Appeal to Men of Reason and Religion* (1745).

the swell of marginalized masses, and they resorted to criminal activity. Wesley's strength was communicating the gospel in "plain words for plain people" with great urgency in the sore places and spaces where they did life. He also unleashed the "plain people," his army of lay preachers, to do it. In an ecclesial ecosystem in which the religious intelligentsia seemingly exchanged "Jesus is Lord" for "Reason is Lord," clergy were overeducated beyond their effectiveness. In many cases, they could no longer connect with the common people. Through small groups, and high expectations that all people would participate and grow as leaders, Wesley helped common people lay a thoughtful theological foundation for their lives.

We now have the great joy and challenge of ministering in a post-Christendom era in the United States. Emerging generations don't speak "Christianese" and typically have no life experience in the church. Therefore, to help people lay a theological foundation for their lives, we must learn to translate our practices into the emerging language of "plain words for plain people." Recovering a "practical divinity" requires comfortability with the "conjunctive" nature of theology, which is centered in a "both/and" mindset. Throughout this book we will see how differing perspectives can be held together in creative tension.

Time for a Remix

It's time for a remix. Most churches in the West have given up the essential early practices that defined our movements. How regularly today are mainline denominations publicly accused of "irregularity," "innovation," "enthusiasm" and generally being "big with mischief" for stirring up the rabble in the fields? How many Baptist pastors today die in jails for placing allegiance to Jesus over allegiance to flags, presidents, and governments? Have we traded in our narrative of a gutsy, boisterous commitment to Jesus as Lord for the narrative of the US corporation? Have we exchanged saddle sores and field preaching for white boards, board rooms, and PowerPoint presentations? The US corporate narrative was a perfect bedfellow for the church in a Christendom scenario in which the Eurotribal church enjoyed the privileged center of society. However, those corporate days are fading. We need the practices and theological commitments of the early church, but they will take new forms on the frontier of a network society.

At the simplest level, a "network is a set of interconnected nodes."[4] So, these networks of technologically enabled flows of multimodal communication connect in real physical and digital localities that Castells calls "nodes." A node could be anything in a specific network, from a city, to a restaurant, to a park, to a laptop, to an iPhone screen. The nodes are the connection points determined by the network. For instance, the nodes of a financial network may be an auto debit paycheck deposited in a banking site, to an e-trade account on a home personal computer, to a stock market exchange, then cash coming out of an ATM. The nodes of the illegal drug trade network that penetrates economies, states, and societies across the world could be "coca fields and poppy fields, clandestine laboratories, secret landing strips, street gangs, and money laundering financial institutions."[5]

So, what does this look like in our everyday life? We most likely live in a place, our home, apartment, condominium, and so on. But our home is also a "node" in a larger network. We surf the web, Facetime, and send emails that have global implications at the speed of digital light. A friend through one of our social media sites (Facebook, X, Tik Tok, or Instagram, for example), invites us to a local coffee shop tomorrow afternoon. The coffee shop is a node where other networks interact. For instance, a yoga group is using the front porch, a group of entrepreneurs is convening in the back room, also connected here by the digitally enabled flows. (We will unpack the "space of flows" in the next Download). The shop owner makes credit card transactions that travel as digital currency into the flows

4. Manuel Castells, *The Rise of the Network Society* (Oxford and Malden, MA: Blackwell, 2000), 501.

5. Castells, *The Rise of the Network Society*, 501.

that connect a larger global financial network. Many networks are interacting in one location, all participating in a larger network of connections. Right at your local coffee shop!

In the liminality or "in-betweenness" of our time, as society itself moves through this fundamental change, we are transitioning into the post-industrial, knowledge-based era now described as the Information Age. One important aspect of this transformation as noted is *globalization*. Moynagh and Worsley define globalization simply as the world becoming "more interdependent and integrated," with physical, cultural, and virtual dimensions.[6] So technology has made the world smaller and we are now a truly global community. Cultures consist of bundles of dynamic *practices*, connected across space and time through structured flows of information and media.[7] Alan Hirsch describes practices as *embodiments of values*. This is the living out of a culture's assumptions in such a way that they can be observed and experienced by others.[8]

A typical week in the life of a person today involves spending most of the days on screens: phone screens, laptop screens, GPS screens, and flat screens. They may not know their own next-door neighbors but have a network of friends on social media that they meet with for face to face encounter to engage in practices together. Those practices could be a running group, yoga, taking their kids to play sports. They could be centered upon a love for pets, or simply gathering at a favorite Mexican restaurant for burritos and beers.

The web and wireless communications are more than traditional media, they are a global means of interactive, multimodal, mass self-communication. Castells writes,

6. Michael Moynagh and Richard Worsley, *Going Global: Key Questions for the Twenty-First Century* (London, UK: A & C Black, 2008), 1–7.

7. Ryan K. Bolger, "Practice Movements in Global Information Culture: Looking Back to McGavran and Finding a Way Forward," *Missiology* 35, no. 2: 181–93 (2007), 188.

8. Alan Hirsch and Dave Ferguson, *On the Verge: A Journey into the Apostolic Future of the Church* (Grand Rapids, MI: Zondervan, 2011), 174.

For hundreds of millions of Internet users under 30, on-line communities have become a fundamental dimension of everyday life that keeps growing everywhere . . . on-line communities are fast developing not as a virtual world, but as a real virtuality integrated with other forms of interaction in an increasingly hybridized everyday life.[9]

Thus, the distinction between real and virtual made by more chronologically mature generations is changing in the network society. Virtual reality is reality. Also, the idea of defining oneself by a locality is a fading phenomenon. Due to the power of mobilization and technologically enabled flows, we may work in one city, go to school in another town, gather for communal practices in several, and yet live in another.

Len Sweet writes, "People today congregate not on shared streets but around shared interests."[10] Communities of practice are groups of people who share a common passion for an activity and grow in the performance of that practice as they interact regularly over time. The practice could be as complex as tattooing, or as simple as gathering for coffee, reading together at the library, or taking your dog to the dog park. Later I will discuss what the Church of England as defined as "pioneer ministry." These pioneering Jesus followers live incarnationally in micro-communities gathering around a multitude of possible interests in a wide array of contextual variations. Within those practices, they, "through shared actions and words, point to the kingdom in such a way that the practice itself moves towards God."[11]

Donald McGavran was sent to India as a missionary in 1923 by the United Christian Missionary Society of the Christian Church (Disciples of Christ). He became a missiologist and founding Dean of the School of World Mission at Fuller Theological Seminary in Pasadena, California.

---

9. Castells, *The Rise of the Network Society*, xxix.

10. Leonard I. Sweet, *Me and We: God's New Social Gospel* (Nashville: Abingdon Press, 2014), 17.

11. Bolger, "Practice Movements in Global Information Culture," 189–90.

Known for his work related to evangelism and religious conversion, he is widely regarded as the most influential missiologist of the 20th century.

The missiological DNA of Donald McGavran has been rightly associated with the Fresh Expressions movement.[12] After thirty-two years on the mission field in India, McGavran wrote *The Bridges of God*. There he explains how "Peoples" become Christian rather than simply "individuals," which he sees as the primarily Western individualistic approach to Christianization. He describes layers or strata of society and how people are often confined within their own intimate stratum.[13] He argues that a people is not simply an aggregation of individuals but a "social organism." The attractional only church mode (build it and they will come) can also be extractional, marked by personal conversion of the individual, followed by their removal from the social organism and placement in the new social organism: the "mission station" (for our purposes, the church compound).[14]

McGravran proposes that "extraction," removing someone from that social organism, is exactly the wrong thing to do. This does violence to the social organism and actually defeats the larger missional purpose. He notes a phenomenon called "group mind" in which individuals don't understand themselves as a self-sufficient unit but part of a group. Peoples are Christianized as this "group-mind is brought into a life-giving relationship to Jesus as Lord."[15]

Peoples become Christian through a chain reaction, a wave of decisions for Christ, sweeping through the group mind, which McGavran calls a "people movement." These groups are usually small in number, but

---

12.   Louise Nelstrop and Martyn Percy, *Evaluating Fresh Expressions: Explorations in Emerging Church: Responses to the Changing Face of Ecclesiology in the Church of England* (Norwich: Canterbury Press, 2008), 38.

13.   Donald A. McGavran, *The Bridges of God: A Study in the Strategy of Missions*. Eugene, Ore: Wipf & Stock, 2005), 1.

14.   McGavran, *The Bridges of God*, 8–11

15.   McGavran, *The Bridges of God*, 8–11

through a series of small groups being instructed in the faith over a period of years, large numbers of new Christians can manifest.[16]

McGavran's missional approach has suffered major criticisms—particularly the Homogenous Unit Principle (HUP), which states that in subsections of society, members of those subsections who have some characteristics in common prefer to become Christians without crossing racial, linguistic, or class barriers.[17] However, missiologist Ryan Bolger reminds us that these critiques are more reflective of McGavran's American "translators" who in the 1990s hijacked and twisted his concepts to grow suburban megachurches.[18] Later, I will explain the missional approach Bolger calls a "practice movement," which is McGavran's "people movement" remixed for a network society.

Vincent Donovan was a Roman Catholic priest who served as a missionary to the Masai people in Tanzania for seventeen years during the 1960s and 1970s. He also saw that the highly individualized Western approach of evangelizing people one by one is ineffective. Donovan too struggled with what he saw as an "extractional" approach. He saw that the dominant missional paradigm created communities of outcasts, now dependent on the church and unable to impact their social group. Typically, *communities* of people become Christian or they don't at all. Donovan's evangelistic efforts among the Masai demonstrated that people are indeed converted at the level of a homogenous unit.[19]

Fresh expressions form among groups of people who are a "workable community," often connected by some ritual, place, or hobby. These are living social organisms distinct from other social groups. A fundamental premise of the missional church movement is not to extract people from their indigenous communities and bring them back to the church compound for proper Christianization but to help those communities form

---

16. McGavran, *The Bridges of God*, 12–13

17. Nelstrop and Percy, *Evaluating Fresh Expressions*, 38.

18. Bolger, "Practice Movements in Global Information Culture," 182.

19. Vincent J. Donovan, *Christianity Rediscovered* (Maryknoll, N.Y: Orbis, 2003), 64.

church where they are. This enables the church, largely inaccessible to many, to manifest in every nook and cranny of everyday life.

Paul Chilcote writes that the Wesleys in their own day rediscovered what we would call today this "missional church."[20] Wesley became an incarnational presence in the fields, boldly proclaiming the Lordship of Jesus, and inviting hearers to join into that reign. Groups of people for whom the church was largely inaccessible became Christian communities. Today, pioneers incarnate themselves in the new "fields" (the "nodes" of a network society) and through a loving, relational, withness approach to evangelism, invite communities of people to live together under the Lordship of Jesus.

In a network society, while we are hyper-connected all the time, never have we been more alone. Isolation is the great soul wound of our time. The surgeon general's 2023 report described the social condition as an epidemic of loneliness and isolation. Fresh Expressions of church form organically with groups of people connecting in neutral places around shared practices. The practice itself will be transformed as the disciple seeks to live under the Lordship of Jesus in the micro-community. Other participants in that practice can experience transformation as they grow in their relationship with the Jesus follower.

"Conversion" is less about praying a sinner's prayer and more about obeying the Spirit nudges that occur through the messy relational process around the shared practice. The healing from isolation is a mutual exchange between the disciple and the non-Christian. Contextual churches form, native to that community of practice, as Christians and not-Christians live together in friendship and form a common language. The Holy Spirit is transforming the dispositions of the participants through the waves of grace, as they enter more fully into Jesus's Lordship together.

The emergence of this new form of society necessitates a revolution in the missionary approach in the US. How is Jesus Lord of the network society? How can we be a church not only for our neighborhoods but

---

20. Chilcote, *Recapturing the Wesleys' Vision*, 20.

also for our networks? John Wesley saw the change in his own day, and adapted practices to reach people where they were. This is what the Fresh Expressions movement is allowing us to do today: planting churches or new networked ministries in the wild, with new people, in new places, and in new ways.

We need vintage forms of church to engage our neighborhoods *and* fresh forms of church to engage the networks all around us. Further, one professional clergy person doing the work of evangelism to grow his or her flock is a bankrupt concept. The new missional frontier requires the whole people of God, the "priesthood of all believers." Every Christian may invite others in their relational sphere to live under the Lordship of Jesus. Pioneers are a new breed of "lay preachers" turning their interest and hobbies into forms of church. A new movement of the "common people" is being unleashed.

Field Story
Holy Smoke
Pastor Marlon Mack
Sweet Home Missionary Baptist Church, Gary, IN

The first time I heard of Fresh Expressions was during the enrollment process at United Theological Seminary. I discovered there was a Fresh Expressions House of Study there led by Dr. Michael Beck. Being a part of the National Baptist Convention USA, Inc., we did not have any fresh expressions that I was aware of. Hesitantly, I started to engage the movement. As I began reading the assigned books for the class, I was apprehended by the concept. It was new, fresh, and exciting! I must admit, beyond the books and lectures illustrating the biblical models of Fresh Expressions, something seemed a bit familiar, but I couldn't quite put my finger on it until we shared time in our Intensive in July of 2023.

During our class time and discussions, I realized that as far back as 1994 I had been engaged in and employing a form of Fresh Expressions without even knowing it. Dr. Beck assigned a presentation on *The Blended Ecology of the Church: Why or Why Not?* Upon completion of the assignment and hearing my classmates share their support of and concerns about implementing Fresh Expressions, I KNEW that the Lord was leading me to become a Fresh Expressions Adventurer.

I returned to the Sweet Home Missionary Baptist Church in Gary, Indiana, following the intensive on fire! I was ready to get at it, but the Lord tempered my zeal. I've always said that destiny is the place that opportunity and preparation had a head-on collision. You can be prepared and never get the opportunity, or you can get the opportunity and not be prepared. I knew that if I was going to get the buy in of our congregation, I had one shot, and it had to be my best.

My mind began to think about my community. Where were the people? What were their needs? How could I make this happen? Would the Lord be with us and bless our efforts? Fortunately, it didn't take long for the Lord to answer me. The Holy Spirit told me to look in our pulpit! The newest member of our Ministerial Staff was a brother that I had met, of all places, in a Cigar Lounge! Holy Smokes, that was it! Our first Fresh Expressions venture would be called Holy Smoke, and it would be held at Elements Cigar Lounge (ECL) in Highland, Indiana.

I began peppering my sermons and teachings with the message and methods of Fresh Expressions and the Blended Ecology. Next, I began meeting with members of our congregation to do some initial teaching, not simply on the "whats," but the "hows" of Fresh Expressions. The idea was met with skepticism from some, but many others began to contemplate what they could do in terms of cultivating their own Fresh Expression.

After much prayer, I approached the owners of ECL and explained to them what the Lord was leading me to do. God had gone before me and prepared the way! The people of peace, who were already immersed in the culture and community, were on board! Holy Smoke launched on

Thursday, January 18 at 7:30 p.m. with eleven brothers present! We have been going strong every first and third Thursday of the month.

Currently, we are planning on launching our second Fresh Expression in the Barber Boyz Klub. It will be called either Taper Talk or Faith and Fadez. Our plan is to launch by the end of 2024. We continue to seek God's guidance and favor as we endeavor to increase the reach and enlarge the territory of God's Kingdom.

Missional Field Kit: Forming Your FX Team

The first step in engaging the new fields of a network society is simply gathering together a small group of fellow subversives who will join you in the cultivation of fresh expressions. At one congregation, we there was a handful of people serving on the Evangelism Committee who said, "We're the ones who couldn't get on any of the good committees." Obviously, that's not a very positive perspective! They turned their Evangelism Committee into the Fresh Expressions team, which is now one of the most thriving groups in that church. Later, I'll suggest we need to think of this team as the "disruptive innovation" department of our church.

While it may not start in this way, we suggest your team grow to include people in each of these three spheres:

1. **Core:** solid followers of Jesus, may already be part of your church.

2. **Fringe of the Core:** these are people either new to the life of the church, or maybe not in your church. These folks have relationships in the community and know the landscape of practices there.

3. **Fringe:** these are people outside the life of your church who will be your "persons of peace" (Luke 10:1-12). They may not be Christian, but they open the door to the potential relational networks in your community.

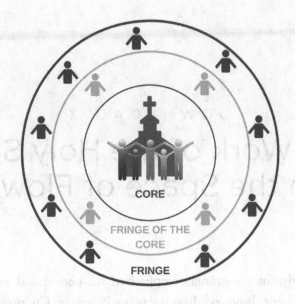

Further, you should also recruit on the team persons who fulfill the three essential roles we will discuss in detail later:

1. **Pioneers:** people who are passionate about mission on the edges

2. **Supporters:** people who are passionate about supporting and releasing pioneers

3. **Permission Givers:** People who use their role to foster release of pioneers and to influence the system to be more willing to experiment

Your team could start by reading Luke 10:1-12 together. This is Jesus's missional blueprint for a pre-Christian world, but it also works for a post-Christian world! Study it. Reflect upon it. Digest it. It will undergird all further work your team will do together. Encourage each person on the team to read through this book and explore the missional field kit exercises together.

The Work of the Holy Spirit in the Space of Flows

The early church strongly emphasized the person and work of the Holy Spirit. Pentecostalism today is a Protestant Charismatic movement that emphasizes direct personal experience of God through baptism with the Holy Spirit. Many branches of Pentecostalism, while diverse, adhere to some form of an understanding for the necessity of the New Birth. But it is often distinguished by belief in the "baptism in the Holy Spirit," which includes the use of spiritual gifts: such as speaking in tongues and divine healing. Pentecostals see the movement as a return to the apostolic age of the early church.

Many trace the modern Pentecostal movement back to William J. Seymour, a Wesleyan-Holiness preacher who taught that speaking in tongues was a sign of Spirit baptism and a third work of grace. The growth of Pentecostalism throughout the United States and the rest of the world seemed to originate with the three-year-long Azusa Street Revival, in Los Angeles, California.

Others say the foundations of this movement trace back further to the Evangelical Revival that swept western Europe in the latter part of the seventeenth century and early eighteenth century. Some are surprised to find the accounts of supernatural occurrences, including speaking in tongues, healings, exorcisms, prophecies, dreams, and miraculous escapes in the ministry of John Wesley.[1] The whole movement was seemingly enabled by the Spirit. Lay preachers, some illiterate, were boldly proclaiming the gospel and ordinary folks did extraordinary things. Chilcote writes, "The Wesleys equated the Holy Spirit—third person of the Trinity—with God's empowering presence."[2]

Paul told the Corinthians that no one can say "Jesus is Lord" except by the Holy Spirit (1 Cor 12:3). The Spirit is the life force that flows through the body of Christ. Furthermore, renewal movements do not sweep the face of the earth by the sheer will power of human beings. Fortunately, we have a "helper" (John 14:16; 16:7) who "guides" us into "all truth" (John 16:13).

This third person of the Trinity is affirmed in the Nicene-Constantinopolitan Creed as the one who "proceeds from the Father and the Son; who with the Father and the Son together is worshiped and glorified."[3] If we follow the sequence of Jesus's incarnation, death, resurrection, ascension, and sending of the Holy Spirit at Pentecost, we realize the Spirit (one with Jesus and yet distinct) makes the presence of Jesus available now. The risen Jesus is not confined to one place, in one moment in time, but has been downloaded into every living thing and permeates the entire cosmos (Eph 1:23). The experience of Jesus's resurrected presence sustained the early church and enabled their confession of his Lordship (1 Cor 12:3).

More precisely, the Holy Spirit is involved in the transformation of the entire cosmos and all living things (Rom 8:22-23). The Spirit is working, healing, and guiding all the universe to a final form of emergence— the new creation (Rev 22).

God the Spirit, the "wild child" of the Trinity, is always "going native." "Yet we hear them speaking in our own *native* languages!" (Acts 2:8 NLT,

---

1. Daniel Jennings, *The Supernatural Occurrences of John Wesley* (CreateSpace, 2005).

2. Paul W. Chilcote, *Recapturing the Wesleys' Vision: An Introduction to the Faith of John and Charles Wesley* (Woodstock, VT: Skylight Paths Publishing, 2011), 92.

3. Quoted in Ted Campbell, *Methodist Doctrine: The Essentials* (Nashville: Abingdon Press, 2011), 44.

emphasis mine). The "subversive one" is a missionary spirit, operating outside the bounds, moving on the missional edge, bringing forth community among division, and enabling humanity to share the very *agape* of Christ.[4] In often prevenient ways, the Spirit is forming one authentic, diverse, peaceable community from all the peoples of the earth. The Holy Spirit is infilling and supernaturally enabling humanity to fulfill God's mission for the redemption of the world. Yet, the Holy Spirit manifests the Kingdom in "native" and "personal" ways. The Holy Spirit is never forcing some cultural perspective on another group of people but emerging out of who and what they already are. It is not the work of the Holy Spirit when missional leaders advance a colonial, attractional, propositional form of Christendom instead of incarnational living.[5]

Elaine Heath reminds us that at times the church has colluded with secular and military power, and "mission and evangelism" have been "hijacked to serve the interests of empire."[6] We have sometimes read the Great Commission in this way. This is an inaccurate depiction of our Christian faith that more resembles a Western narrative of power—a false narrative that deceives us into thinking the answer to most problems is the appropriate application of corporate power. If we use our power to do this, we can overcome that, solve this problem, fix that broken thing, and so on. If we just use our power appropriately, we can "take back our community" for Jesus.

There is profound solidarity across traditions that the ultimate outworking of the Spirit's power is love. This love is a different kind of power—relational power—faithful presence—*withness*. It's also a love that goes first (1 John 4:9). God's love is already at work on the scene before

---

4. Loida I. Otero, Z. Maldonado Pérez, et al., *Latina Evangélicas: A Theological Survey from the Margins* (Eugene, OR: Cascade, 2013), 28–32.

5. David J. Bosch, *Transforming Mission: Paradigm Shifts in Theology of Mission* (Maryknoll, NY: Orbis, 1991), 1.

6. Elaine A. Heath and Larry Duggins, *Missional, Monastic, Mainline: A Guide to Starting Missional Micro-Communities in Historically Mainline Traditions* (Eugene, OR: Cascade, 2014), 12.

we get there. We can't "take back the community for Jesus," because by the power of the Spirit the community already belongs to Jesus.

The Spirit always goes ahead of us and is already intimately involved in the life of every person we encounter. Leaders of the Evangelical Revival became aware of this in their field preaching.. They found the Spirit at work in the lives of people beyond the church walls, inviting them to join what God was already up to. The Spirit was inviting them to "go native."

Because the world truly was their parish, their pulpit took many forms. This example is relevant to the new missional frontier in a network society. Because these leaders believed the Spirit went before them, many places became their *pulpit*. They had church in every conceivable location.

In the emerging industrial revolution of the eighteenth century, field preachers were leveraging the power of first, second, and third places. Not only did they understand the importance of embodying the gospel in the places where people lived, they also had the contextual intelligence to adapt to the rhythms of their lives. For example, John Wesley adjusted his schedule to times when he could reach the people. He preached every day— morning, noon, and night—wherever his voice could be heard by a crowd. He also habitually preached at 5 a.m., so he could catch the workers as they went off to work in the mines, forges, farms, and mills. This was so important to Wesley that he called the early morning gatherings "the glory of the Methodists" and said if this was ever abandoned, "Ichabod" (the glory of God has departed) should be inscribed over Methodist societies.[7]

On one occasion, Wesley discovered the early morning gathering had been abandoned at Stroud. He wrote, "Give up this, and Methodism too will degenerate into a mere sect, only distinguished by some opinions and modes of worship."[8] This foreshadows his more well-known and often quoted statement,

> I am not afraid that the people called Methodists should ever cease to exist either in Europe or America. But I am afraid lest they should only

7. Wood, *The Burning Heart,* 154.

8. Wesley, quoted in Wood, *The Burning Heart,* 154.

exist as a dead sect, having the form of religion without the power. And this undoubtedly will be the case unless they hold fast both the doctrine, spirit, and discipline with which they first set out.

This is an apt description of many churches today. A church without the Spirit is one "having the form of religion without the power." How did we "degenerate" into a Sunday morning attractional-only mode from this? Can we adapt some of these early practices for today?

The Holy Spirit is up to something out in the fields again, stirring up a movement out in the ordinary places where people do life.

Time for a Remix

So how do we "go native" in the power of the Spirit on the new missional frontier of a post-everything society? The fresh expressions movement resembles the early church's deep reliance on the person and work of the Holy Spirit. This seems to have been reawakened in the Pentecostalism sweeping the globe today.

God the Spirit is a trailblazer. Always blazing trails of new creation that leave healing in the wake. *The trailblazing Spirit is calling us to the fields.*

The "fields" have changed. The massive social shifts have literally transformed the human experience of space and time. In a network society, we must now recognize the difference between two kinds of space: the *space of place* and the *space of flows*.

Castells believes that space, throughout human history, has been "the material support of simultaneity in social practice." So, cities for instance, are communication systems, increasing the chance of communication through physical contiguity (direct contact). He calls the *space of place* the space of contiguity.[9] Through the amalgamation of technologies listed earlier, along with computerized transportation, "simultaneity was

9. Manuel Castells, *The Rise of the Network Society* (Oxford and Malden, MA: Blackwell, 2000), xxxi.

introduced in social relationships at a distance" (distanced contact). Meaning, humans no longer need to interact face to face in a physical place to have "contact." This transformation of the spatiality of social interaction through simultaneity creates a new kind of space: *the space of flows*. Castells defines the space of flows as "the material support of simultaneous social practices communicated at a distance."[10]

Castells writes, "The key innovation and decision-making processes take place in face-to-face contacts, and they still require a shared space of places, well-connected through its articulation to the space of flows."[11] Microelectronic and communication technologies serve as *flows* that enable us to connect across geographies and time. "Flows" of capital, information, organizational interaction, images, sounds, and symbols move along a complex web of interconnected networks enabled by these technologies. Flows are the means through which the movement of people, objects, and things is accomplished from one node to another in social space. The network society is an interconnected matrix, activated by these technologically enabled flows. The flows are the social organization, the expression of processes dominating our economic, political, and symbolic life.[12]

Sociologist Ray Oldenburg furthers our understanding of the "space of place," in his description of first, second, and third places connected by flows of technology in a mobile culture. First Place is the home or primary place of residence. Second Place is the workplace or school place. Third Place may be public places separate from the two usual social environments of home and workplace which "host regular, voluntary, informal, and happily anticipated gatherings of individuals." Examples are environments such as cafes, pubs, theaters, parks, and so on.[13]

---

10. Castells, *The Rise of the Network Society*, xxxi.

11. Castells, *The Rise of the Network Society*, xxxvi.

12. Castells, *The Rise of the Network Society*, 442.

13. Ray Oldenburg, *The Great Good Place: Cafés, Coffee Shops, Bookstores, Bars, Hair Salons, and Other Hangouts at the Heart of a Community* (New York: Marlowe, 1999), 16.

These "places" are the "fields" for us today, the "nodes" of a network society. These places are outside the earshot of church bells, where people gather for community. We need soft eyes to notice these Holy Spirit "hot spots," and access the kingdom wi-fi there. In a mobile, hyperconnected, and diverse culture, a neighborhood approach to mission alone will not suffice. We still need an effective missional approach for the neighborhood, focused on a specific people in a stationary place. We need also to cultivate a healthy missional approach for the network that allows us to adapt to the emergent societal structure. This approach unleashes an exploration of endless new avenues for mission, a kaleidoscope of contextual variations for fresh expressions of church which come in all colors, shapes, and sizes.

The trailblazing Spirit goes ahead of us in the space of flows in a network society. Knocking on the doors in the church neighborhood is in many contexts the least effective method to engage people. In the 5G speed of mobile culture, we are experiencing the largest urbanization trend in human history. Overpopulation of cities is leading to the creation of smaller dormitory-like home places, and how people dwell in these living quarters is changing.

Are we really present in our home places when we are physically there? For instance, if I'm in my home in Ocala, Florida, but using FaceTime with my friend in London, what time zone am I in? Or if I'm corresponding through email with a friend in California, am I fully present in Florida? If I'm watching a livestream video of my colleague in Momostenango, Guatemala, leading a prayer march as it unfolds in real time, where is my consciousness? My body could be present as well, since I can literally fly in an airplane, jumping space and time, to any of these places in less than a day. Castells suggests that "computers, communications systems, and genetic decoding and programming are all amplifiers and extensions of the human mind."[14]

---

14.   Castells, *The Rise of the Network Society*, 31.

These technologies literally enable us to be present to some degree across the world at any given moment. A part of us, our technologically extended mind, can actually through the phenomenon of distanced contact be present across vast geographic distances. The technology enables a kind of extension of ourselves to be present on the digital frontier. This leads to the compression and transformation of time, that is "the development of flex-time, and the end of separation of working time, personal time, and family time, as in the penetration of all time/spaces by wireless communication devices that blur different practices in a simultaneous time frame through the massive habit of multi-tasking."[15]

Moynagh and Worsley describe space in the network society as "a world above the world."[16] In the space of flows, Castells speaks of a "timeless time" and a distinction between the "instant time of computerized networks versus clock time of everyday life."[17]

These transformations can have a significantly adverse effect: a disembodied life. Thus, the very nature of a hyper-connected global community creates disjuncture by the loss of commitment to a particular locality. The separation caused by the emerging societal structure leads to *deterritorialization,* which refers to the disconnection between peoples, culture, and place. It means the distancing from one's locality made possible by these flows in virtual, cultural, and physical globalization.[18] If emerging generations are spending ten hours per day on screens, how present are we to the physical environment and people where our bodies are at any given moment?[19]

In a culture where most people don't know their next-door neighbors *physically*, they have vast networks of next-door global neighbors *digitally*.

---

15. Castells, *The Rise of the Network Society,* xli.

16. Michael Moynagh and Richard Worsley, *Going Global: Key Questions for the Twenty-First Century* (London, UK: A & C Black, 2008), 3.

17. Castells, *The Rise of the Network Society,* 506.

18. Ryan K. Bolger, "Practice Movements in Global Information Culture: Looking Back to McGavran and Finding a Way Forward," *Missiology* 35, no. 2: 181–93 (2007), 188.

19. See https://www.cnn.com/2016/06/30/health/americans-screen-time-nielsen/index.html.

Relationships are largely enabled and sustained through flows of communication technology. People connect physically through the flows, across geographies, to engage communal practices in neutral places. These network-based relationships bring healing to our isolation and satisfy our longing for human connection. If we believe the Spirit is at work in the seemingly random encounters of our day-to-day lives, why would we doubt that the Spirit is "going native" through these technologically enabled flows in the digital frontier? Why would we assume the Spirit is not present in the endless variety of contextual practices that relationships form around, such as yoga, dinner parties, soccer fields, coffee shops, and so on?

A networked missional approach is not a fresh concept, as we will see later through the missional approaches of Paul the Apostle. Yet it must begin where all mission should—with authentic relationship, desire to connect with and know and love our others. Any missional strategy that does not begin with an agenda-free love for others is questionable. We need simply to gather with a group of people and engage in the *practice* together, connected by *flows*, in the *places* where they do life.

A primary example of this practice is described in Luke 10:1-9, the missional blueprint of Jesus. The disciples, going out two by two, are instructed to locate a person "who shares God's peace" (Luke 10:6). For the first disciples, this was someone who opened his or her home, welcomed them at the table, and unlocked the relational potential of a community. In the network society, a peace-loving person can also open a network, a community of practice, teach us the language, and show us how things work around here. It is an utterly incarnational approach. We come empty handed as a learner into the world of the other (Luke 10:1-8). We take on a posture of vulnerability, with a single focus on forming a relationship. The Spirit works through that honest desire. If the Trinity is a revelation about God, God's way is a divine dance of loving relational power. The Spirit works through relationship, ushering in the kingdom in new, powerful ways as we reach out lovingly toward one other.

In the Information Age, people move through the digital flows, in a 24/7 work culture at blazing 5G speed. Fresh Expressions practitioners utilize these technologies to create a presence on the digital frontier. Using Instagram, X, MeetUp, and the Metaverse, they are planting new forms of church. Forming or incarnating themselves in micro-communities around shared interests, hobbies, and practices, "nones and dones" are forming relationships with Jesus through these pioneers. This is unleashing once again the whole people of God, a movement among the "common people" in the fields.

Thus, through relationships with real people in the "nodes" (physical places) we spread the Christian faith like a good virus in the entry points that spreads through the "flows" (digital channels of connectivity) and heals the entire global network from the inside out.

Prayerfully seek what and where the Spirit is leading you. Ask what the Spirit is up to in the places where people do life. What are the rhythms of people's lives in our contexts? How are we engaging the neighborhoods of our communities? Also, how are we engaging the complex system of networks? In what ways are we utilizing the flows that connect people across geographies? What are practices in the zip codes within our reach, and how is the Spirit working through these practices to bring people together in relationship? How do we "go native" to join in the fun? Who are the "peacemakers"? Who are the "trailblazers" for whom these practices are native?

Field Story
"God Works Very Surprisingly"
by Erik Verwoerd
Project Leader of Pioneering
for the Protestant Church, Netherlands
Protestantse Kerk (2023)

People in their twenties and thirties talk to each other about important life questions at the pioneering spot LUX in The Hague. Pioneer

Rik Zwalua says, "For young people, the threshold of the physical church building is high. We bring the church to them."

What gives your life meaning? What role does faith play in your daily life? People in their twenties and thirties talk about these kinds of questions at LUX in The Hague. "Century-old questions that still matter," says team member Reitse Keizer. LUX is a pioneering place—a new form of church, intended to reach people who would otherwise not come to church. The Netherlands now has approximately 250 pioneering places within the Protestant Church.

Searching for Something to Hold on To

With various activities—from master classes and book reviews to workshops and meditation moments—LUX invites young people to search together for answers to important life questions. There is room for everyone's views and input.

During table discussions, in small groups of five to eight people, it is about everyone's quest. What gives you strength, and where do others find support, peace and strength? What can you learn from Jesus about what is good and true? Reitse: "The great thing about LUX is that you meet different people. Believer and nonbeliever. Those who ask critical questions and those who like to chew on things. People with *roots* in The Hague and newcomers to the city. Everyone is welcome."

High Threshold

"We started LUX four years ago, as part of the missionary program of the Bethlehem Church in The Hague," says pioneer Rik Zwalua. "We wanted to set up something for people in their twenties and thirties who have just started on the labor market. They mainly work here for ministries and large multinationals. The threshold of the church is often too high for this group. We thought: what if we turn it around and bring the church to the people? This is how LUX started, in the beginning mainly with meetings in cafes and at event locations."

Different World

During Covid-19 times, creative solutions were devised to maintain contact. "In the beginning we couldn't do much," remembers Rik Zwalua. "We quickly switched to the digital path. Then we made a podcast about the question: 'What makes you happy?' We also saw corona as a period to ask yourself big questions, because life really came to a standstill."

The podcast had twenty episodes, which were widely shared in the young people's networks. "All people we didn't know yet," Rik continues. "It's great that even more people heard about LUX!"

Nowadays, LUX meetings are held in a historic church building in the city center of The Hague. That took some getting used to for many young people: you literally enter a different world. But, as Rik experiences: "If the environment is in order and you tailor your language to the living environment of young people, a lot is possible."

Mysterious Way

The constant surprise is what Rik likes most about pioneering work. "I believe that God works in very surprising ways, sometimes in a some-what mysterious or hidden way. At least not the way I expected." He mentions a young woman with whom he struck up a conversation. "She came to our celebrations and became interested. After personal conversations, she developed a desire to be baptized. That happened last summer, in the sea near The Hague. It is so wonderful that we could be a link in her journey to personal faith."

Zwalua underlines the importance of missionary work. "It is important that we free people to shape this work. You can't get a pioneering place off the ground in two years. First you have to invest heavily in building relationships. That is a long-term matter. It takes time, space, and trust to let the gospel reach young people. At LUX we experience that many beautiful things arise!"

Missional Field Kit:
Finding Holy Spirit Hot Spots

Instructions: You need a large white board, or stick up paper, and markers. Gather your team, pray, and read Luke 10:1-12 together. Ask for someone to volunteer as the resident artist. Where are the "fields" (first, second, and third places) that you have access to? These are the "hot spots" of the Holy Spirit. In a network society connected by flows, we are always looking for wifi to "connect." Pray together, try to discern where you can connect and download what the Spirit is up to . . . .

1. Draw your home base.

2. Draw out potential first, second, and third places where people gather.

3. Is there any place on the map where someone on the team goes frequently?

4. Do you have a "peace-making person" in one of these locations already?

5. Prayerfully decide which possibilities have the most potential.

6. Who will take responsibility for the potential locations, networks, people?

7. What's the next logical step?

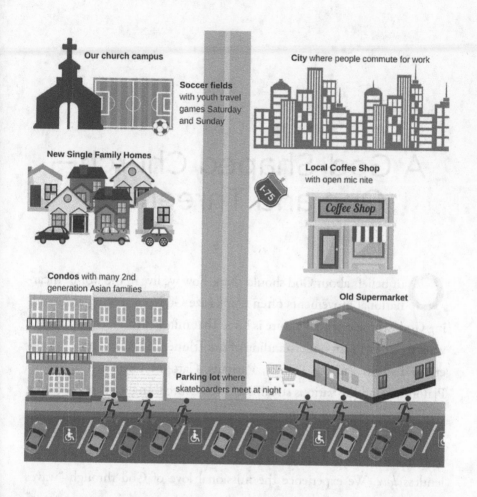

Our church campus

Soccer fields with youth travel games Saturday and Sunday

New Single Family Homes

Condos with many 2nd generation Asian families

City where people commute for work

Local Coffee Shop with open mic nite

Coffee Shop

Old Supermarket

Parking lot where skateboarders meet at night

I-75

A God-Shaped Church— One and Threeness

Our beliefs about God should shape how we live in the world. Incarnational movements often emphasize God as a seeking and sending God, whose essential nature is love. That mindset fuels actions. Here I want to set forth an understanding of the Triune God that weaves together the Eastern Fathers, Pietists, Puritans, Caroline Divines, Cambridge Platonists, and the various streams of high church Anglicanism, blending them into a "practical divinity."

Movement leaders continue to emphasize a personal experience of a *seeking* and *sending* Trinitarian God, whose primary characteristic is relentless *love*. We experience the missional love of God through "waves of grace" (prevenient, justifying, and sanctifying) and "means of grace" (prayer, searching scripture, communion, fasting, and holy conversation). The discipleship process is connected to these means of grace and waves of grace—the profuse outflow of God's unconditional love.

Will Willimon discusses the "processional" or "sent" work of the Trinity, emphasizing the Wesleyan heritage of a "sent" rather than "called" ministry. Being on the move, itinerating from place to place was born from Wesley's dynamic seeking and sending trinitarianism.[1] The Trinity

---

1. William H. Willimon, *United Methodist Beliefs: A Brief Introduction* (Louisville, KY: Westminster John Knox, 2007), 6.

as missionary seeks *and* sends the church. At the conclusion of every worship experience at St Marks Ocala, we observe Holy Communion. We remember at the table how God sought us, put on flesh to get to us, and how Jesus heals the breach in our relationship. Then we turn and face the door as reconciled people for the benediction, the sending forth. I always reiterate that just outside that door is the third largest mission field in the world. Many Americans don't know God lovingly put on flesh in refusal to be separated from them and is available to transform their lives. Thus, every Sunday we remember together that our relational and missionary God has invited us to join this mission (Matt 28:18-20). As God the creator's "sent" people, we as the body of Christ, go out, guided and infilled by the Holy Spirit (John 20:21b-22).[2]

All Christians believe together in one true and living God, infinite in power, wisdom, goodness, and love—God is the creator and sustainer of all things. This relational triune God's oneness is expressed in three Persons, of one substance, power, and eternity.[3] Exodus 3:1-15 describes God's seeking of an orphaned Egyptian fugitive named Moses to send on an impossible mission. God hears the cry of the people, God seeks, and God sends. This portrait of an astonishingly compassionate God who is vulnerable to the pain of people, using a misfit as a chosen instrument, deeply resonates with my own experience of God. I, too, in the presence of an awesomely holy God was relentlessly sought and sent. I, too, cried "Why me? Who am I?" and received the same simple answer, "Because I'll be with you" (Exod 3:12).

I preached a sermon on this passage in the first-person narrative titled "The Worst Man for the Perfect Job." In that sermon, as Moses, I was carrying on a deep conversation about the brokenness of my distant past with the sheep I was herding. Suddenly, God appeared in the burning bush! In my exchange with God, I wrestled with God's self-identification

2. *United Methodist Hymnal*, "Word and Table II," 14. "That we may be for the world the body of Christ."

3. *The Book of Discipline*, ¶103.

as "I am that I am." While there is no space here to explicate the variety of interpretations of this name-formula, "this enigmatic name demonstrates power, fidelity, and presence."[4] Also it is a crucial focal point for the unfolding self-revelation of God's intervening action in history articulated in the scriptures.

God is in an interconnected matrix of relationship we call the Trinity. We seek to understand this relationality within the Godhead as the *perichoresis*—the circle dance of the Trinitarian life. *Perichoresis* refers to the "mutual interpenetration" or the way the three Persons of the Trinity relate to one another. This is an image of God as "community of being" in which each Person although one, remains distinct, penetrates and is penetrated by the other.[5] It is a blending of diversity and oneness. In God's *I Am*-ness, we discover a community of diverse singularity—the three-yet-one.

Incarnational ministry, both in the cathedrals of the established church, and out in the fields, reawakened an understanding of this three-in-one seeking and sending God, whose primary characteristic is active, initiating love. Most ministers across history were deeply locked into an "attractional only" form of church, waiting for non-Christians to stumble into the ranks of their dwindling flocks. This approach misses the central essence of God's seeking and sending nature, and how the church is an extension of God's graceful activity in the earth.

There is another move in God's seeking and sending self-revelation: the outpouring of the Holy Spirit and the sending of the church. The church is quite literally another incarnation of Jesus, the Body of Christ in the world. This understanding of God influenced many denominations view of the church as a "redeemed and redeeming fellowship." Some hold an "instrumental" view of the church. Each of the movements we have explored so far enabled the church in some way to embody both the seeking and sending nature of God—a God shaped church.

4. *Exodus. New Interpreters Commentary: General Articles and Introduction, Commentary, and Reflections for Each Book of the Bible, Including the Apocryphal/Deuterocanonical Books* (Nashville: Abingdon Press, 1994), 714.

5. Alister E. McGrath, *Christian Theology: An Introduction* (Malden, MA: Wiley-Blackwell, 2011), 241.

Time for a Remix

The fresh expressions movement allows the church to recover a robust understanding of the seeking and sending nature of the Trinity. Just as God's own life is a communion in which oneness and diversity are shared in a divine dance of "making room," for one another, so inherited congregations planting fresh expressions cultivate this kind of relational interaction with their larger community. The perichoretic nature of the Trinity demonstrates how in God's own eternal being there is a movement of seeking and sending. Father sends the Son, Father and Son send the Spirit. The Spirit seeks and descends upon Jesus in the murky waters of his baptism (Luke 3:22). The father of the prodigal keeps his eyes on the road, watching for the son, and while he's still a far way off, he runs to him (Luke 15: 20-21). There is a profound giving and receiving of love in which God "makes room."

The Risen Jesus breathes the Holy Spirit on the disciples and says, "As the Father sent me, so I am sending you" (John 20:21). Mission is linked with the Trinity, and this realization gives new life to the modern missional church movement. Mission is no longer subservient to ecclesiology or soteriology. Rather mission is the purpose of church alignment and life together with Christ. David Bosch writes, "The classical doctrine on the *missio Dei* as God the Father sending the Son, and God the Father and the Son sending the Spirit was expanded to include yet another 'movement': Father, Son, and Holy Spirit sending the church into the world."[6] This understanding was embodied in the fields by Celtics, Benedictines, and Beguines. In some ways, it led to the restructuring of the church around the new organizing principle of mission, the outworking nature of God's seeking and sending love.

The recovering of this movemental understanding unleashed the Evangelical Revival in England. The stagnation of the church was stirred to movement again. The scattered groups of people in the fields, miners'

---

6. David J. Bosch, *Transforming Mission: Paradigm Shifts in Theology of Mission* (Maryknoll, NY: Orbis, 1991), 390.

camps, and town squares interacted synergistically with the gatherings of worshippers under their steeples. Over time, the movement was institutionalized, settling the activity in the fields for church sanctuaries. However, this attractional form of church can be separated from mission until it no longer resembles the movemental nature of God.

The shape of the church today can be reflected in the relational dance of the Trinity. If we were to recover the form of the church, as derived from the very *perichoresis* of "interpenetration" and the "community of being," of Father, Son, and Spirit, would this be a God shaped church?

Anglican theologian and professor at St. Mellitus Lincoln Harvey sees the "mixed economy" or what I call the "blended ecology" as reflecting God's very nature.[7] This "shape" of the church, with stationary and emerging modes dancing together, reflects the dynamic, movemental, and loving interrelationship that is the seeking and sending heart of the Trinity. The blended ecology is a demonstration of this flow of mutual giving between the inherited and emerging modes of the church. It creates a dynamic otherness which "makes room." One mode in isolation is a parody of God's nature. Both together, interacting in rhythms of space making, actually draw communities into the life of God. More simply, the shape of the church is derived from the Trinity as missionary—a shape that is both fixed and fluid, the blended ecology.[8]

The Holy Spirit dances between the fresh expressions and the inherited congregation, seeking and sending. The Triune God, a life of shared love, not self-contained individuals, draws the community into that life. Presbyterian theologian and Princeton professor Daniel L. Migliore writes, "just as the life of the triune persons is life with, for, and in each other, so the church is called to life in communion in which persons flourish in mutually supportive relationships with others. In such communion, the

---

7. Lincoln Harvey, "How Serious Is It Really? The Mixed Economy and the Light-Hearted Long Haul," in Graham Cray, Ian Mobsby, and Aaron Kennedy, *Fresh Expressions of Church and the Kingdom of God*, 95–105 (Norwich: Canterbury, 2012), 98.

8. Michael Beck, *Deep Roots, Wild Branches: Revitalizing the Church in the Blended Ecology* (Franklin, TN: Seedbed, 2019).

church becomes *imago Trinitatis,* an analogy of, and partial participation in, the triune life of God."[9]

British theologian, missionary, and author Lesslie Newbigin was originally ordained within the Church of Scotland, then spent much of his career serving as a missionary in India with the Church of South India and the United Reformed Church. He is now considered the father of the modern missional church movement. Newbigin wrote, "The idea that one can or could at any time separate out by some process of distillation a pure gospel unadulterated by any cultural accretions is an illusion. It is, in fact, an abandonment of the gospel, for the gospel is about the word made flesh."[10]

The church is in some sense always shaped by the age in which it's emerging afresh. As we will see more fully, a key principle of incarnational ministry is harnessing the energy of change as society moves through various transformations.

While the church's form has always grown out of its interaction with context, the danger is the corruption of the church by the context. As Swiss Catholic priest, theologian, and author, Hans Küng noted, cultural adaptation is not always good, "for that could mean adapting itself to the evil, the anti-God elements, the indifferentism in the world."[11]

Emerging generations describe the vast disconnect between the Jesus of scripture and the church of North America or Europe. Like it or not, the church lost it's prophetic street cred and backbone. Even more damaging, in the search for political power, we lost our legitimating narrative beneath many layers of corrupt imperial perversions.

Alan Roxburgh discusses at length how Protestant denominations in the US adopted the organizational structure of the twentieth-century corporation and benefited greatly. By adopting this corporate structure,

---

9.   Referencing John Zizioulas, *Being as Communion: Studies in Personhood and the Church* (1985) in Daniel L. Migliore, *Faith Seeking Understanding: An Introduction to Christian Theology* (Grand Rapids, MI: Eerdmans, 2014), 274–75.

10.   Lesslie Newbigin, *Foolishness to the Greeks: The Gospel and Western Culture* (Grand Rapids, MI: Eerdmans, 1986), 4.

11.   Hans Küng, *The Church* (Garden City, NY: Image Books, 1976), 12.

we helped churches to thrive in that season, as the legitimating narrative of United States capitalist culture became a seemingly perfect bedfellow for the church. Churches took up the language of rationalized efficiency, professional management, and bureaucratic structures.[12] The attractional, "build it and they will come" model worked well in a Christendom culture that emerged in the American democracy. However, this societal form is passing into irrelevance as the network society emerges. The hub and spoke, hierarchical structure of the corporation is fading from view. The new shape of society is networked, dispersed, and polycentric.

Once again, we must adapt to the societal shifts taking place all around us at the speed of digital optics. Yet, we need not abandon fixed for fluid, because we live in both worlds simultaneously. We need both forms of church. This both/and way—worshipping in a parish congregation and in the fields—is the deepest narrative of scriptural teaching about the blended ecology.

In the Bible, we find a community defined by Jerusalem *and* Antioch, the gathered *and* the scattered, the inherited *and* the missional, the attractional *and* the contextual. The blended ecology is a life-giving remix. It's gathered *and* scattered, it's inherited *and* missional, it's attractional *and* contextual.

In the Old Testament, on the way to the promised land, God dwells in a tent, a *tabernacle*. God and the community who bears God's name are *missional*—a mobile force moving from place to place on the desert frontier. God also takes up residence for a while in a *temple*—a stationary place, God's primary zip code, where all people would be drawn to worship. God is an *attractional* force in a particular locality, Mount Zion, until the Babylonian captivity, when the people are dispersed, and God's house is destroyed. Then we see the emergence of the *synagogue*, a word that describes both a place and a people. The *synagogue* combined a more localized, contextual space, and held the pilgrimage to the temple as an

12. Alan J. Roxburgh, *Structured for Mission: Renewing the Culture of the Church* (Downers Grove, IL: InterVarsity, 2015), 79.

expectation. We see how this both/and arrangement functioned in Jesus's own life in each of the Gospels.

In the New Testament, there is a compelling portrait of the blended ecology evidenced again by Jerusalem *and* Antioch. The first Jerusalem council offers us a model for how the blended ecology can work together in a synergistic way (Acts 15). Jerusalem, representing the inherited church, confers to decide what to do with a swell of Gentile converts in Antioch, the emerging church. Jerusalem, as the attractional center in continuity with Israel, decides to support, embrace, and guide what's happening in Antioch. Antioch decides to collaborate and be in relationship with the "institution," if you will. Antioch is a very different contextual form of church. It is an indigenous manifestation of the context, with very different ideas, different language, and different people. The two modes learn to live together, and the rest is history.

THE BLENDED ECOLOGY

Acts 15:

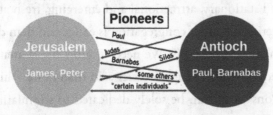

Modern:

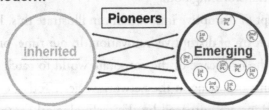

This image illustrates the interactions we see in Acts 15, and the modern form of pioneers moving between the two modes. We will explore this more fully in the next download.

Perhaps the most compelling image of this both/and way is centered in the incarnation of Jesus himself. Jesus's own life and ministry included synagogue and temple, coexisting together. Jesus worked in the fields of his day, while also teaching (and instigating holy mischief) in the temple. He embodied the church among the people, on mountain sides, lakes, front porches, and in the synagogues. Jesus, the most *attractive* human being that ever was *and* the manifestation of God's *missional* heart was the embodied fulfillment of temple, tabernacle, and Torah. His body itself was the new temple or tabernacle (Luke 22:19; John 2:19). Jesus was the stationary, mobile, enfleshed, incarnational, attractional, emerging flesh-and-blood tabernacle, temple, synagogue—fully human, fully God, one. Now the church is the continued embodiment of Jesus, "the body of Christ" (1 Cor 12:27) and "temple of the Holy Spirit" (1 Cor 6:19).

To be a *God shaped church* is to be one and diverse, seeking and sending, mobile and stationary, attractional and emerging, fresh and vintage.

Re-engineering an entire congregation is easier said than done. Fortunately, we don't need to do this! We need to grow the center and experiment on the edge—which is again easier said than done. This is where a "fresh expressions" team can be solely dedicated to stimulating this missional activity. The activity of this team will eventually feed back into the congregation, transforming both.

The concept of disruptive innovation can illustrate this. Field preaching served as a form of disruptive innovation. In our time, one need only briefly survey the landscape of the corporate world to catch a glimpse of the massive shifts occurring in the network society. Today, even the most agile organizations are outpaced by the technological forces revolutionizing the world around us in real time. One significant mistake can lead to a death-dealing scenario. Small entrants are able to take advantage of these shifts to harness emerging technologies to displace large, powerful, established incumbents.

Littering the North American business world are the tombstones of companies that were unable to stay on the edge of innovation. Companies that are frequently used as illustrations here are Blockbuster, Kodak, and Borders Group. In some sense these entities were transitional, meaning they utilized interim technologies. They are now just a few examples of once great organizations that epically failed to adapt or tried to hold on to early success. The interim technologies they utilized were simply replaced by forces of technological innovation, propped up by tax free laws or subsidies beyond their control.

Blockbuster passed on an opportunity to purchase Netflix; instead they were bankrupted by them. While Kodak actually developed the first interim version of digital cameras, companies like Canon rode the wave of the digital image revolution. The Borders Group of bookstores: Waldenbooks, Borders Express, Borders airport and outlet stores, had opportunities to expand into the online market but fell off the innovational edge and were essentially steamrolled by Amazon. Some would add Christian denominations among the tombstones of has-beens.

In the *Harvard Business Review*, Clayton Christensen (et al.) clarifies some common misconceptions about disruptive innovation. Essentially, they define the phenomenon as a process where smaller emerging companies challenge established corporations by harnessing innovative technology. Established corporations tend to focus on their most profitable existing customers. Most of their energy, creativity, and effort are around improving their products or services for those existing customers. In that focus, incumbents place themselves outside the purchase capability of poorer, overlooked segments. Entrants then simply target those overlooked segments, which proves disruptive for the incumbent.[13]

13. Clayton M. Christensen, Michael E. Raynor, and Rory McDonald, "What Is Disruptive Innovation?" *Harvard Business Review*, December 2015. Accessed October 20, 2017. https://hbr.org/2015/12/what-is-disruptive-innovation.

For example, why go to Blockbuster and rent materials that I will most likely return for a late fee, when I can have all those rentable materials streamed into my home for one low monthly fee with Netflix? No searching the aisles, seeking to locate the prefect movie for my family only to find an empty box. No "be kind, rewind" campaign.

So, the entrant can focus on functionality of a product or service at a lower price. Larger corporations cannot typically respond efficaciously to the disruption, which goes mainstream by engaging a larger segment for a more reasonable price. In that scenario disruption has occurred.

By comparison, when early adopters like George Whitfield took up "field preaching," a disruptive innovation occurred. He began to reach a mass segment of the population that the larger church was not reaching. The institutional fixation on buildings, education of clergy, and caring for the wealthy members of the church allowed the Evangelical Revival to thrive among the poor. While the larger church was targeting a smaller segment of already Christians, Whitfield was targeting the masses of uneducated working-class people. He went to the miners' camps, debtors' prisons, and street corners where the people lived. He got out in the "flows." He then manifested the church in the neighborhoods and networks of the emerging industrial society, circumventing the bureaucracy of the attractional model.

It's not hard to see that much of the current institutional church is targeting a "high end market" of educated people with money, and more specifically catering to the needs of already Christians. While God loves this people group and they should certainly be a focus for the church, we are often missing the bigger picture. The Western churches' strategy is focused on a false assumption, that there are Christians out there who need a good church. The demographic of those who identify as Christian is decreasing every year, while the population grows massively. We are overshooting vast segments of the population, fighting for the little population of already Christians. That's why Fresh Expressions aims to reach the "nones and dones." Just as disruptive innovations originate in low-end or new markets, so the emerging missional movements are putting the church in the places where people do life together—livestreamed right into their relational living rooms, so to speak. The focus is not attracting Christians from other congregations, it's reaching new people who don't go to church.

Our advisers in the *Harvard Business Review* remind us, "'Disruption is a process.' The term 'disruptive innovation' is misleading when it is used to refer to a product or service at one fixed point, rather than to the evolution of that product or service over time."[14] For example, we see that process actually unfold in the early insurgent forms of Christianity that crisscrossed the fledgling American colonies. It's not about creating a product or giving birth to new denominations; it's a process to reach overlooked segments of society.

Some of the largest, most successful corporations are getting ahead of disruptive innovation by creating departments that make disruptive innovation the focus of their experimentation and development. "Our current belief is that companies should create a separate division that operates under the protection of senior leadership to explore and exploit a new disruptive model."[15]

This business analogy compares to what a fresh expressions team can accomplish in a congregation. The inherited congregation provides the rooted depth and focuses primarily on care of existing members, while the emerging micro-communities serve as the research and development branch. We can have our corporate structure and a disruptive innovation department operating together in a symbiotic, life-giving way. Most if not all of our energies in the current paradigm are focused on caring for the members of a congregation. As a local clergy person, this can easily consume my whole week if I let it. However, many churches die in the process of being cared for by their pastor. We need to do both: care for the center and stimulate the edge.

14. Christensen, Raynor, and McDonald, "What Is Disruptive Innovation?"

15. Christensen, Raynor, and McDonald, "What Is Disruptive Innovation?"

We looked at the examples of Blockbuster, Kodak, and Borders Group, and how corporations like Netflix, Canon, and Amazon harnessed the disruptive innovation to flourish while the older established companies stuck to their business plans.

One of the massive implications of a disruptive innovation is that it allows the one harnessing its revolutionary force to gain access directly to the consumer. The disruptive innovation process typically harnesses a technology that circumvents the current structures and bureaucracies. When this occurs, it changes the market and the entire system has to respond to the innovation. Forward-looking, proactive organizations can harness the energy, ride the shift, and capitalize on the new emerging scenario. Rigid institutions that misunderstand their own purpose and base their identity in how they have been successful in the previous market will ultimately fail.

This is where Jesus's forgotten beatitude is of the utmost importance: "Happy are the flexible, for they won't get bent out of shape." (I know Jesus said this somewhere, but nobody wrote it down.)

Unfortunately, the US church has not been very flexible or more precisely, not very responsive to the disruptive innovations all around us. We have lost the improvisational, responsive, highly adaptive model of the early church, and fallen more into the institutional hierarchy.

Fresh Expressions is a form of disruptive innovation. It puts us directly in the living rooms, running groups, restaurants, fitness clubs, tattoo parlors, and social spheres where people are doing life together, connected by flows. Jesus loves the people of those communities, and he created the church as an instrument to reach them. We have something to offer humanity: a revolutionary force of love that can change their lives forever. It's something the church alone can give. We must rekindle the innovative nature of the primitive church to reach people in fresh ways.

Fresh expressions springing up in the first, second, and third places interact synergistically with the inherited church. Pioneer teams are sent out into the community as instruments of God's seeking love. The local church becomes an equipping and sending hub for these local missionaries. The life of the church spills into the community; the community spills into the church. "Church" is no longer confined to a compound where people gather for a regular rhythm, but Jesus communities are springing up everywhere throughout the larger communal ecosystem. Every place becomes a potential "burning bush" where the seeking "I Am" God of Moses is calling fugitives into a relationship.

This allows the church to reflect the *shape* of the Trinity. The church is the people God has sought and sent as "temple of the Holy Spirit" and "body of Christ" in the world. This enables a recovery of the "priesthood of all believers" that we will explore more fully next.

Here's a glimpse of what a blended ecology ecosystem in the network society can look like.

THE BLENDED ECOLOGY ECOSYSTEM

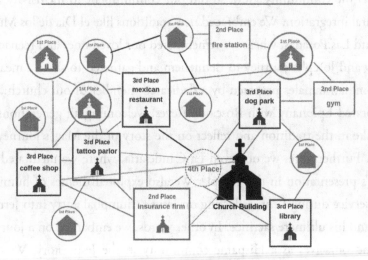

Field Story

Andrés Pérez González
Brazos Abiertos UMC
Geensboro, NC

The story of transformation at Brazos Abiertos UMC, a Hispanic faith community in Greensboro, North Carolina, is both ordinary and extraordinary. What began as a small gathering of immigrants and refugees seeking solace and community has blossomed into a vibrant and inclusive fresh expression of church that continues to impact lives in profound ways. The journey of Brazos Abiertos UMC started with a simple vision: to create a safe haven where people could wrestle with their faith, grow in community, and experience the transformative love of Jesus. This vision became a reality less than a year ago on a Sunday afternoon, as a couple of people gathered in a classroom to share pan dulce and engage in a sermonic conversation.

As the community grew, so did our commitment to inclusivity and cultural integration. We embraced new traditions like el Dia de los Muertos and Las Posadas, where we remembered our loved ones and reenacted Mary and Joseph's journey to Bethlehem and gathered to share a meal of Colombian tamales prepared by a dedicated member of our church. We celebrated Epiphany with Rosca de Reyes, welcoming all generations to partake in the tradition and reflect on the story of the Magi's journey of faith. Furthermore, we observed La Candelaria, where we meditated on Jesus's presentation in the Temple. We also explored themes of humility and service during Lent, reflecting on Jesus's triumphal entry into Jerusalem and his ultimate sacrifice. In other words, we embarked on a journey to find ourselves as a Hispanic community in the Jesus story. We empowered leaders to lead the sermonic conversations and shape the structure of our meetings, allowing them to claim ownership of the space they were building with us. We realized that it was easier for people to pour themselves into this new endeavor because it became theirs as much as it was ours. We became a community.

In one of our recent meetings, where close to thirty people were in attendance, we welcomed a new refugee family from Guatemala. As we introduced ourselves and shared our own immigrant stories, we created a space of understanding and empathy. After the introductions, I invited our people to share their thoughts about Brazos Abiertos and what this community has meant for them. Marian, one of our young mothers, immediately jumped in, "My home," she said, "Brazos Abiertos has become my home," embodying the sense of belonging and warmth that our community strives to offer. This moment exemplifies how our community is starting to embody the ethos of Brazos Abiertos, embracing people beyond mere welcome and allowing them to belong before they believe. This moment of welcoming encapsulates the essence of Brazos Abiertos— a place where strangers become family, where stories are shared and hearts are opened. As Brazos Abiertos continues to grow and evolve, it remains both a fresh expression of church and an attempt to reclaim a Latine/Hispanic way of doing church, embodying the transformative power of holy accompaniment and active solidarity.

Missional Field Kit: 50/50 Evaluation

A helpful principle that enables a church to become "God Shaped" is the 50/50 principle. On the new missional frontier, local churches need to spend half of their time caring for the existing congregation, and half of their time engaging the larger community. This means half of our time cultivating Jerusalem (traditional, stationary, gathered), and half of our time cultivating Antioch (emerging, mobile, scattered). This principle must be embodied by the senior clergy leader, the staff, and every member of the congregation. Here are two field kit tools to get you started:

Field Kit 1: 50/50 Planner

This is a tool for scheduling days in quarters and mapping out the 50/50.

Step 1. Make a copy of the 50/50 planner for everyone on the team.

Step 2. Designate one day as Sabbath, a 24-hour period (for example, from 5:00 p.m. Thursday to 5:00 p.m. Friday or all day Saturday).

Step 3. Optionally, also designate another day as a day off for work and family.

Step 4. Take the remainder of the work week and fill in the thirds with work. Divide those blocks evenly 50/50 between internal work in the church and external work in the community.

Step 5. If you have staff, or a key leadership team, encourage them to do this same exercise with their time.

Step 6. Make these schedules available for the whole congregation. You may even want to designate where you will be in the community on various blocks in the calendar.

Step 7. Encourage the entire congregation to restructure their weeks in the same way. How many hours per week do they devote to serving God through the church (after work, school, Sabbath, and so on)? Can they divide those hours in the following way: half spent in service to the traditional congregation, and half spent in service to the larger community? If they are willing, have them turn in their planners.

50-50 PLANNER		
8AM - 12PM	**12PM - 5PM**	**5PM - 9PM**
MON		
TUES		
WED		
THURS		
FRI		
SAT		
SUN		

© 2017 Fresh Expressions | US

Field Kit 2: Church-Wide Evaluation

With your church leadership, using the 50/50 planner data, evaluate how much of your weekly time is dedicated to Jerusalem (your inherited congregation) and how much to Antioch (missional engagement with your larger community). Have a conversation about this.

A New Priesthood—
Pioneer Ministry

In 1517, a German priest, professor, and Augustinian friar came to reject several teachings and practices of the Roman Catholic Church. His major point of contention was the practice of indulgences (a way to reduce the amount of punishment one must undergo for forgiven sins). Martin Luther attempted to challenge what he believed to be inconsistencies by first proposing an academic discussion, the Ninety-Five Theses. This displeased Pope Leo X, and in 1520 he demanded that Luther renounce all of his writings. Luther refused and was excommunicated in January 1521. In that same year, Holy Roman Emperor Charles V condemned Luther as an outlaw at the Diet of Worms. Luther died in 1546, as an excommunicated priest, but not before his ideas helped spark a movement that today we call the Reformation.

Earlier I mentioned that a Roman Catholic Reformation had already been simmering for at least a hundred years prior to Luther. Consider Italian activists Catherine of Siena (1347–1380) and Catherine of Genoa (1447–1510), working among those in poverty and the *Devotio Moderna* (Modern Devotion) movement to reclaim a greater commitment to the religious life. Girolamo Savonarola (1452–1498), a Dominican monk was executed for challenging the church.

A general council convened in Rome from 1512 until 1517. This gathering, called the Fifth Lateran Council, agreed to make various reforms. It adjourned shortly before Luther came along with his Ninety-Five Theses. Pope Paul III, whose papacy was embroiled in scandal, recognized the Society of Jesus in 1540. Led by Ignatius of Loyola and six companions, the Jesuits took an incarnational approach that unleashed a movement of evangelization and apostolic ministry that has spread to 112 nations.

And yet, Luther's rediscovery in the Bible of the doctrine of justification by faith alone was nothing short of revolutionary. This core idea had implications for a whole array of doctrinal beliefs and practice. One key implication was a critique of the hierarchal clergy caste system. If salvation is granted to all those who trust in Christ alone, then there should be an equality among believers. The doctrine of the priesthood of all believers was a natural implication of the doctrine of justification by faith. And while Luther himself never actually used the term "priesthood of all believers" he did describe a "general priesthood of all baptised Christians," and he repeatedly referred to baptized believers as "priests."[1]

Every baptized believer who has faith in Christ share in Christ's royal priesthood. Every Christian has equal access to the Father through Jesus. Thus, every believer has the responsibility to act as a priest to other believers, to be in ministry with our neighbor, and particularly to proclaim the Scriptures.

John Calvin (1509–1564) the leading French, second generation, Protestant reformer, also taught that all Christians are permitted to share in a priestly status and service before God in his *Institutes of Christian Religion* (1536). At only twenty-six years old, and as a relatively new convert, Calvin began writing this work of systematic theology, which remains one of the most influential pieces of Christian literature ever produced. Calvin called for the democratization of spiritual authority under the universal kingship of Christ, while still valuing the role of ordained clergy in

---

1. Uche Anizor and Hank Voss, *Representing Christ: A Vision for the Priesthood of All Believers* (Downers Grove, IL: InterVarsity Press, 2016), 18.

teaching and administering the sacraments. For Calvin, the priesthood of all believers emphasized the calling of every believer to serve God in daily life and vocation. This tension is held together in a covenant theology that equally emphasizes the liberation of the individual and mutual submission within the community.

The people called Methodists were born from an evangelism imperative rather than a doctrinal dispute. Not only did the first Methodists adapt to the emerging changes of society to reach people in the fields, they connected them in a process of discipleship to journey through the life of grace together. This imperative required an army of dedicated laity to sustain the movement. Thus, through solid biblical interpretation, and in some ways through sheer missional necessity, Wesley affirmed the "priesthood of all believers" and the baptismal vocation of all Christians. Lay persons (men and women) led the various Methodist gatherings, because they were gifted by the Spirit for ministry in the church, and as they matured and studied they became the itinerant preachers.

> Converts were trained to become soul-winners themselves. Many enlisted as lay preachers—some itinerant and others local. Many were appointed as leaders in their own society, and in addition to watching over their own flock, engaged in evangelistic activity in the neighbourhood."[2]
>
> One of the most revolutionary features of the Wesleyan revival was its liberation of the laity for leadership, and its blurring of the lines between clergy and lay when it came to priestly functions and spiritual guides. Wesley didn't worry about qualifications since he trusted on-the-job training and expected all Methodists to be lifelong learners.[3]

As demonstrated earlier, revolutionary lay movements have long been a part of the Catholic Church and has often been accomplished primarily through Confraternities, Associations, and Societies. In January of 2022, Pope Francis took a significant step in expanding lay ministry as he

---

2. Arthur S. Wood, *The Burning Heart: John Wesley, Evangelist* (Minneapolis: Bethany Fellowship, 1978),194.

3. Leonard I. Sweet, *The Greatest Story Never Told: Revive Us Again* (Nashville: Abingdon Press, 2012), 79.

conferred the ministries of catechist, lector, and acolyte upon laymen and women in St. Peter's Basilica. The implications of this revolutionary decision are yet to be fully comprehended.

Some of the factors that stunt church vitality today include professionalization of the clergy, lack of leaders indigenous to a particular context, depression of the small-group system, and the diminishment of equipping of the laity for mission. Obviously, lay persons are active in congregations, but in many places their efforts are limited to serving on a committee, leading as a liturgist, or filling in for the preacher a couple of times per year.

Those among emerging generations who want to be engaged with the church are longing for more. They want to be involved in mission, meeting human need, and changing the world, but often have no desire to prop up declining institutions. While future lay leaders may be averse to "membership" or commitment to a single organization, they are more than willing to join in and collaborate with organizations that are making a positive impact in communities.

Time for a Remix

In the global ecosystem, missionary teams are cultivating Jesus communities through the space of flows in a network society. In the Fresh Expressions movement that has emerged in the UK, missionaries have been labeled as "pioneers" because they are particularly adept at moving through the liminality (dislocation, ambiguity) of our age.

Leonard Sweet and I have noted the problematic nature of the term "pioneer" in the United States. While originally Middle French in origin (*pionnier*: a foot soldier, or trench digger), from the same root as peon or pawn, the word "pioneer" for indigenous people connotes the violence, manipulation, and oppression of early European settlers. We suggest a shift in the metaphor from pioneer to adventurer.

The word "adventurer" is rooted in the word "advent," which means "the coming" or "the arrival" of something fresh and new. This is exactly who Jesus' followers are—advent makers, advent markers, advent risers, advent storytellers of adventure. The Latin word *adventus* is the translation of the Greek word parousia, commonly used to refer to the Second Coming of Christ. For Christians, Advent is less a season of the year than an adventitious mindset and an "adventual" lifestyle. Christians are on an adventure between the three appearing's of Jesus, past, present, and future.

Here I will utilize the pioneer language we have inherited from the Church of England, as it is currently the most accepted term ecumenically speaking, and the primary term of the Fresh Expressions movement literature and research I'll be citing.

Three essential roles thrive in the fresh expressions movement: pioneers, supporters, and permission givers. This provides a way for every participant (including non-Christians) to be involved in mission. When these roles work together in alignment, congregations that have been sedentary for a period can rejoin a movement again.

Pioneers are passionate about mission on the edges.

Supporters are passionate about supporting and releasing pioneers.

Permission Givers are people who use their role to foster release of pioneers and to influence the system to be more willing to experiment.

In the United Kingdom, fresh-expression leaders reorganized the entire ecclesial system to make room for *pioneer ministry*. Persons called by God and gifted by the Spirit for pioneer ministry can do so in a lay, licensed, or ordained capacity.

A clear correlation is observed between pioneer ministers and business or social entrepreneurs. They share essential characteristics. While some are bothered that the term *entrepreneur* is used in business literature, we already use business conceptual language in the church: manager, boards, strategic goals, vitality metrics, quality control, and so on.[4] In *Entrepreneurs: Talent, Temperament and Opportunity*, Bill Bolton and John Thompson define an entrepreneur as "a person who habitually creates and innovates to build something of recognized value around perceived opportunities."[5]

Pioneers share many of these traits: they start new initiatives, organize relational networks, innovate, and create fresh things out of existing pieces. They do so in the power of the Spirit.

The Church of England defines pioneers as "people called by God who are the first to see and creatively respond to the Holy Spirit's initiatives with those outside the church; gathering others around them as they seek to establish a new contextual Christian community."[6]

The Church of England also identifies two "types" of pioneers, largely based on "from where" the pioneering happens:

- **Fresh-start Pioneers** (or edge pioneers): These are classic pioneering types who start new things, love firsts, and enjoy working from a blank canvas. If ordained, they need to be released from expectations of an incumbent parish role and allowed to pioneer in places where the Church is not present while remaining closely connected with the diocese.

- **Parish-based Pioneers** (or mixed-economy pioneers): These pioneers want to work from a parish base but from there develop fresh expressions of church in a mixed economy by expanding the growth and reach of the local church.[7]

---

4. David Goodhew, Andrew Roberts, and Michael Volland, *Fresh!: An Introduction to Fresh Expressions of Church and Pioneer Ministry* (London, UK: SCM Press, 2012), 143.

5. Bill Bolton and John Thompson, *Entrepreneurs: Talent, Temperament and Opportunity* (New York: Routledge, 2013), 72.

6. David Male, "Do We Need Pioneers?" 2017. https://freshexpressions.org.uk /get-started/pioneer-ministry/.

7. Male, "Do We Need Pioneers?"

As illustrated below, edge pioneers are already out in our communities and we need to join and learn with them. Mixed-economy pioneers are already sitting in our pews and we need to identify and release them.

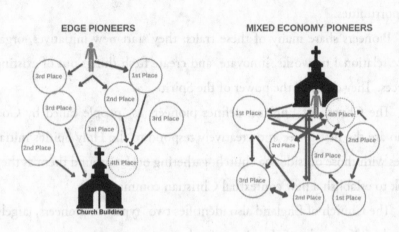

As we find our way through the ambiguity of the current paradigm shift, pioneers function like border-stalkers by moving in and out of the network tribes, bringing hope and reconciliation as they move through the different flows and practices. Among the space of flows and the space of places, these border-stalkers don't claim ownership of any sphere among the networks. They empty themselves in the space of the *other* and incarnate God's love within that sphere.[8]

The theological underpinnings of pioneer ministry are rooted deeply in the Trinity. *God is a pioneering God; thus, there are pioneers.* The church is to be one and diverse, in the way the Trinity is one and diverse—distinct persons, living relationally in a mysterious interdependence, full of

---

8.   *Mearcstapa* (literally, mark-stepper, a boundary walker) or "Border-Stalker" is an Old English term from Beowulf: those who moved between the ancient tribes, living on the edges of their groups, moving in and out, bringing back good news, helping fragmented cultural tribes find hope and reconciliation. Makoto Fujimura, *Culture Care: Reconnecting with Beauty for Our Common Life* (New York: Fujimura Institute, 2014), 39.

creative diversity. The relational interpenetration of the Trinity, always making room for the other, is the embodiment of sending, seeking love.

Each person of the Trinity is a "pioneer." As David Goodhew writes in *Fresh!*,

> God the Father is a pioneer: "God, by the creation of the cosmos, pioneers a new form of reality."[9]
>
> God the Spirit is a pioneer: the Spirit breathes forth all life. Freshness is the hallmark of the Holy Spirit. The Holy Spirit is the "foundation for fresh expressions, pioneer ministry, and church planting." The Holy Spirit is "God as Pioneer Minister—through whom all pioneer ministry finds its authentication and strength." The Spirit "creates community." Thus, the church is a pioneer community of the Spirit.
>
> God the Son is a pioneer: he is the author and instigator of our faith, the one "innovating by who he is (incarnation) what he does (ministry) and by how he dies (cross) and rises again (resurrection)."[10]
> The Trinity is a pioneer team!

Perhaps the most helpful exercise in our task of understanding and unleashing pioneer ministry comes from the pioneering of Jesus. Hebrews 12:2 (NRSV) reads, "looking to Jesus the *pioneer* and perfecter of our faith" (italics mine). Here Jesus is identified as the ἀρχηγός (pronounced är-khā-gos), which means "pioneer" or "author" and conversely "instigator." This term is the closest we get in Koiné Greek to "innovator" or "entrepreneur." God bestows the pioneer upon the church for nurture, upbuilding, and expansion. Paul the Apostle is perhaps a textbook example of a pioneer. Pioneers seek to embody this initiator, starter ministry of Jesus in the world. In the same way, we embody the ministry roles of apostle, prophet, evangelist, shepherd, and teacher (Eph 4: 11).

Jonny Baker observes that pioneers have "the gift of not fitting in." Pioneers are those who have the uncanny gift to see and imagine different possibilities than the accepted ways of doing business as usual, and then

9. Goodhew, Roberts, and Volland, *Fresh!*, 25.

10. Goodhew, Roberts, and Volland, *Fresh!*, 24–31.

build a path to make real this possibility.[11] This can certainly make them unpopular in more conventional circles.

George Lings reserves the term *pioneer* for "originators of fresh entities," while discussing the differences between pioneer-starters and pioneer-sustainers.[12] In his research, he notes the following characteristics:

- A correlation between Apostle and Pioneer;

- Eagerness to "go first" with low risk-aversion;

- On the "edge," always going out to the edge of some new territory to survey the terrain;

- Habitually "create, start, initiate" (which correlates with entrepreneurs);

- Draw followers and are followable;

- Willing to "leave" (move on when the task is done);

- Movers (opposite of static persons);

- "Are met by Jesus" (have usually encountered the Risen Christ at some point)

- Prefer to be with outsiders;

- At home with "signs" (semioticians, context/sign readers, also embrace the miraculous, and supernatural);

- Flexible strategists (employ effectual reasoning, experimentation, improvisation, and intuition);

- Disturb the peace. Some are not easy for more conventional folks to be around because their presence is threatening and difficult for intuitionalists;

---

11. Jonny Baker and Cathy Ross, *The Pioneer Gift: Explorations in Mission* (Norwich, UK: Canterbury, 2014), 1.

12. G. Lings, "Looking in the Mirror: What Makes a Pioneer" in David Male, *Pioneers 4 Life: Explorations in Theology and Wisdom for Pioneering Leaders* (Abingdon: Bible Reading Fellowship, 2011), 31.

- "Bicultural," always formed by and at home in at least two cultures (age, race, nationality, geography, and so on);

- Translators (between times, cultures, peoples, contextual theologians);

- Developers (they activate others and enable them to continue the work);

- Prophetic (they see what is yet unseen and then act: "dreamers who do");

- Can accept suffering and can expect to join Jesus in carrying his cross.[13]

Pioneers often face mutiny, challenges, and cross-carrying. Because of their proclivity to challenge systems and go first in new initiatives, they often do so with arrows in their backs. Most pioneers bear the scars of friendly fire. Three additional characteristics apply to the Fresh Expressions movement:

- Pioneers cultivate fresh expressions (often with little to no resources).

- Pioneers fail forward (fail frequently but keep going).

- Pioneers come in all shapes, sizes, races, and ages; they are not just young, trendy, rebels. (Some pioneers are children and teens and some are in their eighties.)

Hodgett and Bradbury, in their research on pioneers from the Church Mission Society, suggest that pioneering needs to be understood as a spectrum:

1. Pioneer innovators: refers to sodal or "sobornistic" pioneer leaders who, with their teams, venture out beyond the edges of the church's structures to explore the creation of faithful expressions of Christian life among people of a new context.

---

13. Lings, "Looking in the Mirror," 30–43.

2. Pioneer adaptors: refers to those who have the creative gift to adapt these innovations to their own contexts and take the established church's rituals and rhythms and adapt them into new environments.

3. Pioneer replicators: refers to those situated in contexts in which replication is applicable, where a context is seen to be sufficiently comparable so that a successful model of church can simply be repeated.

4. Pioneer activists: refers to those whose gift and vocation is to shape a place in ways that seek to align a community, network, or industry with the values of the Kingdom. They see themselves as missionaries but without the express intention of planting a church.[14]

In the following diagram, I have contextualized the pioneer spectrum specifically for the Fresh Expressions movement in the US, which includes some of our own replicable models: Dinner Church, Church @ Play, and Café Church.

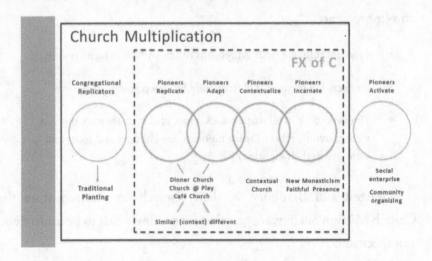

Gerald Arbuckle discusses the reality that though creativity can exist in organizations in a latent way, these ideas require application through

---

14. T. Hodgett and P. Bradbury, "Pioneering Mission is . . . a spectrum." *ANVIL* 34 no. 1. https://churchmissionsociety.org/resources/pioneering-mission-spectrum-tina-hodgett -paul-bradbury-anvil-vol-34-issue-1/

innovative people, who he calls "dreamers who do." He distinguishes between innovators and adaptors:

> Both are creative persons and needed, especially the innovative and refounding type; both threaten the group because they dissent from the acceptable ways of doing things, but it is the innovator that particularly endangers the group's security...[15]

Pioneers can cause a reorganization of the local church. Beth Keith, in "The Gift of Troublesome Questioning," draws a further comparison between adaptors and stabilizers. By their very presence, pioneers threaten overly stable systems by asking "What if?" Stabilizers operate in the impulse to immediately stabilize the disruption. While both have positive and negative attributes, stable systems often support stabilizers only and exile adaptors. Pioneers are gifted by the Spirit to ask troublesome questions that threaten the stability of the system. Pioneers have the ability "to question aspects of the church without drawing the church into question."[16]

Overly stable systems dampen innovation; overly destabilized systems devolve into chaos. Pioneers have a way of destabilizing systems enough to open the organization to the possibility of change. The innovation journey requires some disruption and dissatisfaction. Pioneers are a gift to the church in this way.

Pioneers do not fit neatly into our theological pigeon holes. Their activity and effectiveness challenge the "closely defined liberal, evangelical, or catholic theologies and churchmanship" and they move us "towards something unknown and developmental, with an emphasis on mission, diversity, dialogue and evolving belief and practice."[17]

When intentionally identifying and developing a gifted pioneer, whether in a church, fresh expression, or a formal academic theological setting, consider that pioneers learn in the process of doing, through

---

15.   Gerald A. Arbuckle, *Refounding the Church: Dissent for Leadership* (Maryknoll, NY: Orbis, 1993), 109.

16.   B. Keith, "The Gift of Troublesome Questioning" in Male, *Pioneers 4 Life*, 57.

17.   Keith, "The Gift of Troublesome Questioning," 56.

experimentation and improvisation. Training pipelines are often apprentice-based learning systems. Mature pioneers often possess keen contextual intelligence and become astute contextual theologians, particularly as they gain refined critical-thinking skills that come from depth of education within a particular theological stream.

This can cause denominations to rethink training systems, which usually involve vetting someone theologically and psychologically (by institutional stakeholders) as we let them in and deploy them to congregations. To truly embrace candidates with the pioneer gift, we need to make room in the approval system for them to experiment.

This blending of innovation and sound teaching, driven by the missionary Spirit, challenges some ministry boards, because ministry pioneers tend to have a contextually-formed theology, or a theology shaped while living in a different branch on the Christian tree. Pioneers typically struggle before ordination boards, and once included they are often denied seats in decision-making processes. Pioneers are typically not diplomatic and have impatience with the political maneuvers of the institutional church. Because of their "sharp edges" and the "gift of not fitting in," it's easy to write off their questioning or brainstorms as mad ramblings. The Church of England wisely created the Pioneer Assessment Panel, which consists of a group of established pioneers who evaluate incoming pioneers.[18]

The activity of pioneers can create "institutional confusion." The "typical institutional response exhibits stabilizer tendencies and the inability to adapt old data in the light of new experience. The lack of permission to engage in transformative critique may hinder pioneers' abilities to imagine new possibilities."[19] So the tendency then is for the church to select and authorize the "safe" pioneers who will play well with the system, not question common church assumptions, *and* still develop new forms of church. Unfortunately, this is an unreasonable expectation. Thus, denominations

18. *Vocations to Pioneer Ministry,* https://www.cofepioneer.org/assessment/.

19. Keith, "The Gift of Troublesome Questioning," 58.

often eject the very persons gifted by the Spirit with the adaptation skills that could bring actual revitalization.

There is an ongoing conversation around whether pioneers are born or made. Angela Shier-Jones finds it important to understand a pioneer not as a particular sort of person but as a particular sort of ministerial conduct or focus within the wider framework of the church.[20] All Christians are called to follow the great pioneer, Jesus; this will always include being involved in pioneering. All people created in the image of God have the capacity to start new things. Yet, certain people are particularly gifted to be effective in that particular focus of ministry.

Not all people are pioneers, yet all people can be involved with pioneer ministry. Through creating and leading pioneer academies, I've seen first-hand that pioneers possess a distinct kind of tacit knowledge and naturally display this "ministerial conduct" through a certain set of behaviors or skills. Some disagree with Angela Shier-Jones, arguing that pioneers are indeed a sort of person with inherent characteristics and personality traits that can be identified with sound personality tests.

In my experience, the most prominent trait of a pioneer is simply *confidence*. Pioneers believe they can start new things. They seem gifted to do so. Yet, if pioneering is a gift, it can also be a curse. Hebrews 12:1-2 indicates that when we follow in the slipstream of Jesus's pioneering, enduring a "cross" is par for the course. Further, if everyone were a pioneer, the world would devolve into utter chaos! Can you imagine a church of all adaptors and no stabilizers? Or can you imagine a church where everyone is exactly like Paul? Or if Paul had no Barnabas, a companion encourager (Acts 4:36) who supported him (Acts 9:27), or Ananias, a permission-giver who sent him (Acts 9:17)? So, with fresh expressions, we understand the equal importance of the three roles: pioneer, supporter, and permission-giver.

20. Angela Shier-Jones, *Pioneer Ministry and Fresh Expressions of Church* (London, UK: SPCK, 2009), 3–5.

Perhaps whether pioneers are born or made is the wrong question. Perhaps a more fitting question is *how can we be the church in such a way that every person can be involved in the exciting work of starting new Christian communities?* We find yet another conjunction we must hold in creative tension: every single person can start new things *and* pioneers seem to be especially gifted for this work. This leads us to the more essential truth: pioneer ministry is a work of the body, the whole people of God, and not individual acts of heroic or lone-ranger leadership.

Pioneering is a communal endeavor. Shier-Jones writes, "Pioneering ministry cannot be done to a community by someone who knows what they need; it can only be done with a community by someone who shares in their need."[21] Pioneers are dependent upon the "persons who share peace" and work with the indigenous inhabitants of a community. They must work together with supporters and permission givers in a strategically team-based way, both for the health of the pioneer and the initiatives they start. It's more appropriate to speak of pioneer teams than individual pioneers.

In Download 2, we explored the "space of flows" and the "space of place" in the network society. Physical places serve as "nodes or hubs" in that larger network. So, on this new remixed mission field of a network society, where are the "places" where we can be a "withness"? Where are the missional sandboxes in which pioneer teams play?

The focus on "practices" does not minimize places or people. In fact, the practices and the places are the vehicle through which we form relationships with people. Practices create relational proximity; they enable us to connect in the flows of our mobile social structures. Face-to-face encounter is still the primary place where our isolation is healed. Pioneers raise up indigenous leaders within these communities of practice who in turn raise up more indigenous leaders in the larger web of potential multitudes of networked practices.

---

21.   Shier-Jones, *Pioneer Ministry and Fresh Expressions of Church*, 123.

Pioneers are focused on planting the seeds of the gospel within the fluidity of these cultural flows, connected by the internet, screens, and social media at the speed of digital light. These encounters take place around shared practices in the first, second, and third places of our larger communal ecosystems. One can easily see the potential of this approach, particularly with connecting in the third places around these common hobbies, interests, and bundled practices where they take place.

Here is a refresher:

First Place: The home or primary place of residence.

Second Place: The workplace or school place.

Third Place: The public places separate from the two usual social environments of home and workplace, that "host regular, voluntary, informal, and happily anticipated gatherings of individuals. . . ." Examples are environments such as cafes, pubs, clubs, parks, and so on.[22]

Towns, workplaces, and hobbies exist in a complex web of networked micro-communities. Technology connects people across geographic spaces among those who share common passions. Long ago, community decoupled from locality; it is now centered around leisure, work, and friendships. Technology is now harnessed to connect people in networks, and mobility allows for those networks to transcend locality.

Fresh expressions have tremendous potential in third places. The concept of first, second, and third places was developed by sociologist Ray Oldenburg. Third places are physical, public locations where local residents informally gather to converse with each other. He posited that third places were unique from other public venues because they were places of informal conversation.

---

22. Ray Oldenburg, *The Great Good Place: Cafés, Coffee Shops, Bookstores, Bars, Hair Salons, and Other Hangouts at the Heart of a Community* (New York: Marlowe, 1999), 16.

From *The Great Good Place*, here's a summarization of the shared characteristics of Oldenburg's third place:

Neutral Ground—Individuals may come and go as they please, no one is forced to "play the host." Thus, individuals can visit without a sense of obligation.

Leveler—Reduces everyone in the space to a shared equality regardless of rank or class. It's an inclusive atmosphere, typified by downward association in an uplifting manner, where social strata distinctions are leveled; rich and poor, king and pauper, commune as equals.

Conversational—The atmosphere is informal. Jovial discourse is the main activity.

Accessibility—People can easily access the place beyond normal working hours. Third places often keep late or early hours. Also, they are typically proximally close to the first and second places of our normal rhythms. Proximity and convenience are keys to this accessibility.

Regulars—The grassroots community forms among fellow patrons, not something management provides. The regulars provide the sense of conviviality. Like in the television show *Cheers*, it's a place "where everybody knows your name."

Low Profile—The physical space does not refocus attention away from interpersonal communication. The focus is on relaxation and support that fosters feelings of acceptance.

Playful—The persistent mood is one of playfulness. Leave your overly serious attitude at the door.

Home—This place glows with the warmth of home, it truly becomes a home away from home.[23]

---

23. Oldenburg, *The Great Good Place*, 20–40.

The church once embodied the accessibility and neutrality central to third places in many US communities. In some rural locations, this is still the case. But across the North American landscape, the church largely no longer exists as a third place for the surrounding neighborhoods. For emerging generations, the church is another kind of secret-society lodge, where a peculiar group of people gather to enact strange rituals and use coded language. For many, it is not a viable space to gather and form community.

While in some sense the beauty of a third place has become lost in the relentless work-anxiety cycle of our postmodern culture, understanding how mobile human community forms regularly in these places is essential to our missional task. The formation of community around practices, if albeit sometimes momentarily, is indeed the space of places where pioneers play.

The power of harnessing these third places to form communal life with Jesus is evidenced by the diversity of fresh expressions emerging among the wide array of common practices that take place in accessible, neutral, inclusive, conversational, spaces. As we saw earlier, practices may include tattooing, yoga, kayaking, running, burritos, pets, coffee, tai chi, and the list goes on ad infinitum!

However, to be clear, fresh expressions of church are not merely about places or practices; they are about people: love of people. The guiding questions are not: Do I love this place? Do I love this practice? The questions are: Do I love "the regulars" of this place? Do I love the people who participate in this practice? Rather than asking: Do I love burritos, ask: Do I love the people who love burritos? Not Do I love tattooing, but Do I love the people who find tattooing to be the external artistic expression of their inner lives? Not simply Do I love yoga, but Do I love the people who practice yoga that may or may not have any connection with the church?

This is a remixed form of McGavran's "people movement" discussed earlier, but it is centered on these communal practices. Bolger defines "practice movements" as a missional approach that focuses on the activities that bind people to each other in time and space (i.e., practices). Place becomes secondary to the social space of connections enabled by micro-electronics-based information and communications technologies. Diverse peoples flow in and out of practice-centered communities. These movements involve pioneering Christ-followers who engage these practices through establishing an incarnational presence within the common community.[24]

So then, fresh expressions live in a continual tension of openness to others and a radical call to discipleship. They exist primarily as "centered-set" communities which practice belonging before believing.

THE BLENDED ECOLOGY ECOSYSTEM

How Pioneers Move Through the Five Spheres

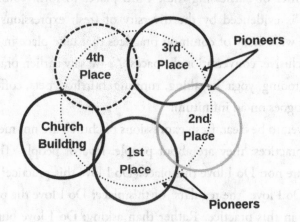

We noticed at Wildwood that many people who connected with us in our fresh expressions of church would eventually visit our Sunday morning services. Many also didn't return. So, for the blended ecology to work,

---

24. Ryan K. Bolger, "Practice Movements in Global Information Culture: Looking Back to McGavran and Finding a Way Forward," *Missiology* 35, no. 2: 181–93 (2007), 189–90.

we needed to create a "fourth place." This is a space in between a fresh expression and a traditional form of church. It's a soft place to land for "nones and dones" who wanted to experience a more traditional form of church. For Wildwood, we call that space "New Life," which is discussed in detail later. Here's a vision of how pioneer teams move through the spheres, bringing others along on the journey:

Notice the distinction of the lines in the diagram, both light and dark, solid and broken; this is a distinction between "bounded and centered" sets. In a bounded-set, a community has clear boundaries, established around beliefs and behaviors, which are patrolled and enforced. One is included or excluded based on adherence. In a centered-set, a community is comprised of non-negotiable core convictions, which are enthusiastically supported and maintained. While an inclusive community, the core convictions shape behavior. One is free to explore moving towards the center, regardless of where in proximity they may be to those beliefs and behaviors.[25]

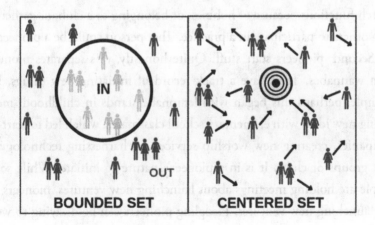

Fresh expressions of church, and particularly the fourth place, operate in a "centered-set" way, rather than as a "bounded-set." They are

25.   Stuart Murray, *Church After Christendom* (Milton Keynes: Paternoster, 2004), 28–31.

communities that primarily follow a "belonging before believing" journey.[26] In a blended-ecology ecosystem, both bounded and centered sets are valuable. The blended-ecology church harnesses the power of both.

Then how do we identify and release pioneers in the missional ecosystems of the local church? If Jonny Baker is correct, and pioneers have "the gift of not fitting in," they will be easy to spot. Shier-Jones, in distinguishing between pioneer ministers and traditional ministers, notes that "they may well present as aggressive, pushy, intense, charismatic and bold rather than accessible, pastoral, supportive, and 'nice.'"[27] In fact, pioneers "smell each other." Pioneers spot other pioneers, and they form strategic partnerships quickly.

You will know pioneers "by their love" or perhaps whom they love, how they initiate community with those they love, and by how they think.

First, a key characteristic of pioneers is that they prefer to be with outsiders. They seem to love outsiders more than insiders. They always have their eyes out for the "other," those who are not "in" yet. Who in your church still has one foot in the world? This person is passionate about a certain people, place, or practice outside the church. He or she misses church functions because of hobbies, or belonging to a club, or gathering with others to participate in a practice. That person could be a pioneer.

Second, pioneers start stuff. Quite honestly, this separates pioneers from wannabes. They have a track record of initiating new things. For example, perhaps this began with lemonade stands in childhood, monetizing new ideas with elementary school classmates, which led to start-up companies, creating new worship services, or harnessing technology to start groups or clubs. It is in a pioneer's nature to initiate. While some people are holding meetings about launching new ventures, pioneers are out launching new ventures. Fledgling pioneers can be dizzying to work with because they are always moving on to the next big idea, the next exciting opportunity, often prematurely. As pioneers mature, they learn to

---

26. Murray, *Church After Christendom*, 71.

27. Shier-Jones, *Pioneer Ministry and Fresh Expressions of Church*, 122.

work through teams and help communities value and adopt their ideas. They learn to create cultural change, and form communities of settlers who sustain their innovations.

Third, pioneers literally think differently. They employ the effectual reasoning typical of entrepreneurs. The word *effectual* is the inverse of *causal.* Causal rationality starts with a pre-determined goal and seeks to develop strategic steps toward meeting that goal. Effectual reasoning does not start with a specific goal. Rather, it begins with a given reality and "allows goals to emerge contingently over time from the varied imagination and diverse aspirations of the founders and the people they interact with."[28]

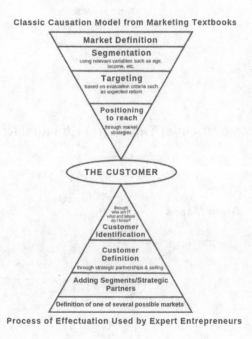

Classic Causation Model from Marketing Textbooks

Market Definition

Segmentation
using relevant variables such as age, income, etc.

Targeting
based on evaluation criteria such as expected return

Positioning
to reach
through market strategies

THE CUSTOMER

through
who am I?
what and whom
do I know?

Customer
Identification

Customer
Definition
through strategic partnerships & selling

Adding Segments/Strategic
Partners

Definition of one of several possible markets

Process of Effectuation Used by Expert Entrepreneurs

28.   Saras D. Sarasvathy, "What Makes Entrepreneurs Entrepreneurial?" 2, https://www.effectuation.org/sites/default/files/documents/what-makes-entrepreneurs-entrepreneurial-sarasvathy.pdf

Managerial Thinking -- Causal Reasoning

Distinguishing Characteristic:
Selecting between given means to achieve a pre-determined goal

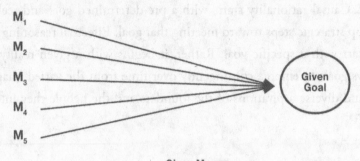

Given Means

Entrepreneurial Thinking -- Effectual Reasoning

Distinguishing Characteristic:
Imagining possible new ends using a given set of means

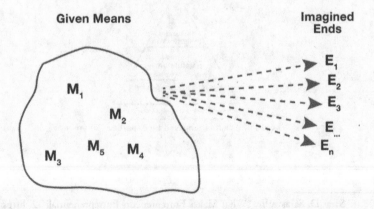

90

For instance, while causal reasoning focuses on expected return, effectual reasoning emphasizes affordable loss; causal reasoning depends upon competitive analyses, effectual reasoning is built upon strategic partnerships; causal reasoning urges the exploitation of pre-existing knowledge and prediction, effectual reasoning stresses the leveraging of contingencies.[29]

Thus, by taking the "effects" and starting with who and what pioneers already have, they begin to create something new from the pieces. Through a series of relational interactions, as opportunities and strategic partnerships arise, multiple outcomes are possible. This kind of reasoning often employed by pioneers and entrepreneurs can fuel a journey of innovation in a traditional congregation.

Who in your community has a history of starting things? Who is always initiating, creating, or having big ideas about what could be? Who is consistently asking troublesome "what if" questions that rattle the guardians of the status quo?

While revitalization begins with a community of leaders in the inherited church, those leaders will need to begin cultivating the emerging forms of church in the community. In the blended ecology, every member can be involved in pioneer ministry; every pioneer team has the capacity to be church planters.

Alan Hirsch has done decades of work on the concept of fivefold ministry or APEST (Apostles, Prophets, Evangelists, Shepherds, Teachers) from Ephesians 4:11-13. Hirsch and others in the missional church movement call for the "recalibration" of the church in the West, explaining how a return to the fivefold ministry as a "primordial form" (one of the meta-ideas that serves as a foundational concept) is essential for the multiplication of the church.[30]

---

29. Sarasvathy, "What Makes Entrepreneurs Entrepreneurial?" 2.

30. Alan Hirsch, *5Q: Reactivating the Original Intelligence and Capacity of the Body of Christ* (USA: 100M, 2017), 19.

Every church needs persons with all five APEST characteristics, to mature to its fullest potential. Fresh expressions give us a process to live this out by releasing the whole priesthood of all believers to plant new forms of church. This is a new generation of bold reformers and itinerant field preachers—a new Reformation remixed for the emerging missional frontier. Pioneers, alongside supporters and permission givers, do this work together. Along with hiring professional church planters, we may need to recognize we have some already in our pews or just outside the walls within our communal sphere of influence.

Blended-ecology pioneers are both/and people; they are border stalkers. However, let's not fall into the misconception that pioneers are solo acts; mature pioneers understand that pioneering is a work of the body. They not only initiate new things, they organize relational networks to sustain their innovations. Who in your congregation or community exemplifies these characteristics? You need those persons on your team.

Field Story

Dr. Dwight Zscheile, Vice President of Innovation and
Professor of Congregational Mission and Leadership
Luther Seminary, St. Paul, Minnesota
Stories from The Episcopal Church

Cook@Church, Rural Suffolk, UK

Cook@Church started in a tiny village in a rural area northeast of London where there are many retirees. These elders gather with youth in a village hall approximately once a month on Sunday evenings where they teach the kids how to cook and practices of table etiquette. There is a fun and playful spirit to the gatherings. Between courses, people are invited to write prayers on slips of paper and place them in a bowl. If the person would like the prayer request to be read aloud, they fold the paper; if they want just the leaders to pray later, they scrunch up the paper. Parents of the youth/children are asked to be involved by praying for it, rather than running it. (It is run by a team of Christian leaders in collaboration with the retirees.) Local councils (local government) are providing grants because they see Christians fostering community and mentoring relationships that otherwise wouldn't take place in the village.

Jesus Fit, Eau Claire, Wisconsin and Minneapolis, MN

Jesus Fit is a beer church that meets monthly in brewpubs to create a space for people to bring their spiritual curiosity and questions without judgment or shame. Participants are invited to name their "soul goals." The focus is primarily on conversation at tables. Jesus Fit is engaging people disconnected from traditional church.

Messy Church (started in UK but now in thousands of locations worldwide)

Messy Church is a gathering for families with young children, typically monthly on a Sunday afternoon. It includes a craft or art activity that relates to a biblical theme, very simple prayers and songs, and a simple shared meal afterward. It is characterized by a spirit of play and creativity, with a highly participatory ethos and tolerance for noise, movement, and children being themselves!

Jesus, Jazz and Dessert Wine, Raleigh, NC

Storyteller Alexus Rhone leads gatherings in downtown Raleigh for spiritual but not religious people that feature jazz music, dessert wine, and storytelling with a spiritual focus. The event is held periodically in a community art space, near where local art crawls happen.

Hot Chocolate (H2O), Dundee, Scotland

H2O started when a small group of church volunteers went out to meet young people in downtown Dundee—that was their only agenda.

They took hot chocolate with them and the young people started called the encounters "Hot Chocolate." The church members got to know them and found out the young people wanted a rehearsal space for their thrash metal bands and a place to hang out. They began to use the church space and to gather around a dinner table three times a week. Over twenty years, this ministry has evolved to include multiple generations of youth, many from disadvantaged backgrounds. It has multiple dimensions of engagement for youth otherwise disenfranchised from church and other institutions.

Seeds of Hope, Ipswich, UK

St. Mary's Stoke is a church founded in 1300 in the small city of Ipswich on the eastern coast of England. The membership was aging and shrinking. The neighborhood has become socioeconomically distressed in recent decades. The church started a "top-up shop"—a food bank where neighbors can shop for a small fee. Before the food bank opens, people are invited into an adjoining room for Seeds of Hope—a simple, fifteen-minute time of prayer, sharing a story from the Bible, and reflection, led by a lay leader. It is optional. Over time, some of the people who come to Seeds of Hope are migrating into Sunday worship. The congregation is now much more diverse than before and has young children.

Missional Field Kit:
Interest Surveys—
Identifying and Releasing Pioneers

To cultivate fresh expressions from the base of the local church, we need pioneers.

One way to identify these people is simply to survey what interests, hobbies, and practices the people in our relational spheres may participate in each week. What do they do for fun, recreation, and community? Later we will help give some suggestions for how those practices can become forms of church.

Prepare a survey or bulletin announcement or email, with the following four simple questions:

1. A pioneer is someone capable of taking the church outside the walls and who can relate or interact with the people there. Do you consider yourself a pioneer, and if so, are you willing to serve on our team?

2. What are your hobbies, interests, or passions, that is, what do you love to do in your spare time?

3. What "networks" of people outside the church are you involved with? What groups do you participate in? (for example, quilting, golf, fitness, bingo, clubs, civic organizations, communities, and so on)

4. What places do you frequent every week? Where do you like to hang out?

Remember that pioneers come in all shapes, sizes, ages, and races. With your team, have a conversation about the survey results and start recruiting.

See a sample survey on the following page.

5 QUESTION
INTEREST SURVEY

PLEASE CIRCLE & FILL IN

FIRST NAME

_____

LAST NAME

_____

PHONE NUMBER

_____

EMAIL

_____

ARE YOU WILLING TO JOIN THE FRESH EXPRESSIONS TEAM?

YES

MAYBE

NO

OTHER

_____

© 2017 Fresh Expressions US

1. HOW FAMILIAR ARE YOU WITH FRESH EXPRESSIONS?

A. Never heard of it
B. Aware of it but need some more info
C. Relatively familiar with it
D. Love it, can't wait to get started!

2. WHAT IS YOUR INTEREST LEVEL IN FRESH EXPRESSIONS?

A. Not interested at all
B. Interested but timing is wrong
C. Interested but need some training
D. Want to be a key leader in this movement

3. WHAT ARE YOUR HOBBIES, INTERESTS AND PASSIONS? WHAT DO YOU LOVE TO DO IN YOUR SPARE TIME?

4. WHAT "NETWORKS" OF PEOPLE OUTSIDE THE CHURCH ARE YOU INVOLVED WITH? WHAT GROUPS DO YOU PARTICIPATE IN?

(ex. quilting, golf, fitness, bingo, clubs, civic organizations, communities etc.)

A pioneer is someone capable of taking the church outside the walls and who can relate/interact with the people there.

5. DO YOU CONSIDER YOURSELF A PIONEER? IF SO, ARE YOU WILLING TO DO SOME TRAINING?

YES   NO   MAYBE - I NEED MORE INFO

Masterpiece Beneath the Mess—A Journey of Grace

W ho knew an orphaned child could birth a grace-filled theology that would one day change the world. As a child, Jacobus Arminius (1560–1609) lost both his parents. His father died suddenly, leaving his wife a widow with small children who was then later killed during the Spanish massacre at Oudewater in 1575. Arminius was adopted by Theodorus Aemilius, a priest with an inclination toward Protestantism. By the grace of adoption, Jacobus became a Dutch Reformed minister and professor in theology during the Protestant Reformation period. His views would become the basis of Arminianism and the Dutch Remonstrant movement.

Arminius sought initially to defend Calvinistic predestination but began to doubt aspects of Calvinism, particularly unconditional election, the nature of the limitation of the atonement, and irresistible grace. He began to speak of "preventing" (or prevenient) grace that has been conferred upon all by the Holy Spirit. This grace was initiated by God, was sufficient for belief in spite of our corrupt nature, and was available equally for the elect, and the non-elect alike.

Although John Wesley knew very little about the beliefs of Jacobus Arminius, he arrived independently in profound theological alignment with him. Wesley was strongly against the doctrines of Calvinistic election and reprobation, while also maintaining that he was within a "hair's breadth' of Calvinism." Wesley acknowledged late in life, with the 1778 publication of *The Arminian Magazine*, that he and Arminius were in general agreement.

This theological system become known as Wesleyan Arminianism, and for 500 years a version of it has been the theological posture of billions of Christians including those in the Wesleyan-Methodist tradition, Anglican, Assemblies of God, Church of God, Foursquare, and many Baptists. The diversity of influential adherents include Richard Allen, Barbara Heck, Ellen Gould White, Jarnea Lee, Sojourner Truth, Phoebe Palmer, Billy Sunday, A.W. Tozer, Billy Graham, Aimee Semple McPherson, D.L. Moody, Oswald Chambers, C.S. Lewis, Charles Finney, and Rick Warren to name a few.

One gift of Wesleyan Arminian theology is its starting point. Rather than beginning with "total depravity" and a sin warped humanity that is helplessly bad. The starting point for a Wesleyan understanding of salvation is a humanity created in the image of God and called "very good." This is held in tension with our current dis-eased state, resulting from original sin.

At Wildwood, I once preached a sermon titled "Masterpiece Beneath the Mess" to flesh out a Wesleyan understanding of salvation. Standing before the congregation on an easel was what appeared to be a framed art piece, totally obscured with washable paint. "What if I told you that beneath this mess was the most valuable masterpiece ever created? More valuable than Raphael's *Sistine Madonna* or Michelangelo's *Creation of Adam*, or any da Vinci, Monet, or Picasso ever made? What if I told you that I knew a master of restoration who could heal any masterpiece? Even this mess." I then began to share from Genesis, about the "very good" nature of God's creation, of which human beings are "supremely good" among all created things (Gen 1:27-31). Let me hold off on the conclusion of that sermon for now.

Human beings are fundamentally relational beings, created to live in loving relationship with our triune God. In "The New Creation" Wesley stated, "there will be a deep, an intimate, an uninterrupted union with God; a constant communion with Father, Son, and Holy Spirit." [1] To be a "new creation" or enter "heaven" is to enjoy an unbroken relationship with God. In fact, the vision of new creation is a remix of the first creation. Humanity already enjoyed this relationship. In God's vulnerable love, God created humanity with the ability to choose or reject God's relational nature. Humanity exercised this gift called free will in the wrong direction, severed that relationship, and unleashed devastating consequences on all of creation (Gen 3). We are all carriers of this wound, the "original trauma." Thus, the *imago Dei* (image of God) became marred, broken, and obscured by sin.

A Wesleyan Arminian understanding of humanity requires holding four key concepts in tension: creation, sin, grace, and law. Grace is the center of the doctrine. It begins with the grace of creation, "very good." Yet, that original goodness is fractured, and healing grace becomes necessary in relation to inbeing sin. [2] Charles Wesley sings "Take away our *bent* to sinning" (italics mine). [3] We are warped, bent, and in a sense deformed by sin. We are in need of redemption, a redemption we cannot accomplish for ourselves. We need to be re-formed from our sin-bent state. The original wound needs healing. Thus, we need grace. Furthermore, we need a healer: God incarnate in Jesus Christ.

First, God's relational love is seeking us, calling out "Where are you?" (Gen 3:9). Saint Augustine speaks of "preventing" grace, arguing against Pelagius, that the first move in salvation is initiated by God. [4] Arminius

1. John Wesley, "The New Creation," *The Standard Sermons in Modern English*, ed. K. C. Kinghorn (Nashville, 2002), 102.

2. Randy Maddox, *Responsible Grace: John Wesley's Practical Theology* (Nashville: Kingswood, 1994), 75.

3. "Love Divine, All Loves Excelling," no. 384, *United Methodist Hymnal*, stanza 2 (emphasis mine).

4. Saint Augustine in *Documents of the Christian Church* (Oxford: Oxford University Press, 1999), 60.

drew from Augustine here. Preceding conscious awareness, God is after us, relentlessly pursuing us, protecting us. Realizing that great love then moves us to accept our brokenness and engage God's transforming grace (Rom 2:4; 1 John 4:19).

The entire "way of salvation" from a a Wesleyan perspective reveals what Randy Maddox calls "responsible grace."[5] God wants to restore us fully to the divine image, God's pre-fall masterpiece, and enable us to completely love God and neighbor. Yet, this does not occur passively. Our life becomes a lived "response" to God's grace. Our development requires some faith work on our part. As James reminds us, faith is dead when it doesn't result in faithful activity (Jas 2:17). Wesley believed this movement along the "way of salvation" marks our lives in a special way. We grow in both personal and social holiness along this journey of grace through the "means of grace."

Our identity as Christians necessitates belonging to a community of accountable discipleship.[6] The true genius of the early Methodist movement was not only reaching people in the "fields" but inviting them into an intentional discipleship process that helped them along the journey of grace.

John Wesley believed that entire sanctification, perfection in love, is achievable in this life. Love of God and neighbor is the ultimate goal but it cannot be accomplished in isolation. It was the genius of the small groups that helped create a system in which people could journey in the power of the Spirit through the life of grace. Methodists with their lives now ripe with the fruit of the Spirit (Gal 5:22-23), could bear the marks of an authentic Christian life, including faith, hope, and love (1 Cor 13:13).

As I concluded the "Masterpiece Beneath the Mess" sermon, I used a rag to wipe away the junk that was obscuring the masterpiece below. As I wiped away the covering paint, I described the process of restoration. I emphasized the Wesleyan understanding of grace manifesting in primarily

---

5. Maddox, *Responsible Grace*, 83.

6. Dietrich Bonhoeffer, *Life Together* (New York: Harper & Row, 1954), 21.

three waves. God's prevenient grace is calling us, wooing us, meeting us in the mess, never giving up. Christ's atoning work makes available the justifying grace, which redeems us and begins our regeneration. Then, by sanctifying grace, the Spirit is continually restoring us into the very fullness of God's image. As the shiny, mirrored surface began to appear, I lifted up not a piece of framed art but a mirror.

The listeners beheld their faces in the reflection as I walked among the congregation. I explained that each of us has also been obscured, marred by the consequences of sin (Gen 6:5; Rom 3:10, 23; Isa 64:6). Just like that mirror, we are powerless to remove the junk for ourselves. If we understood that every life was a priceless masterpiece of God in the graceful process of restoration, perhaps it would help us truly love. Jesus is our healer, lovingly wiping away the confusion, the chaos, and the clutter. The Spirit is continually polishing us into Christ's image throughout our lives (Rom 8:29).

Time for a Remix

The creative starting point of our missional posture in fresh expressions is "supremely good." We believe "goodness" is baked into every layer of creation and every person within it. Like a cake, the fundamental ingredients of God's universe are epic goodness, beauty, and truth of massive proportions. We get to go on a treasure hunt in our communities to identify and play forth these ingredients, showcasing them for all to taste. We search for the beauty, truth, and goodness already there, and collaborate with God in their cultivation. This profound goodness is also in every person, yet sometimes we need to look harder. God is already present in every place and every individual where we go. And yet, there are other forces at work as well.

Catholic theologian and healer Father Richard Rohr emphasized the connection between the Big Book of Alcoholics Anonymous and the Gospel in *Breathing Under Water: Spirituality and the Twelve Steps*. Rohr believes the Twelve Steps of Alcoholics Anonymous are America's most significant and authentic contribution to the history of spirituality. He sees the steps as an accessible version of the Christian faith, which provides a manageable design for life in a broken society.

Rick Warren and John Baker of Saddleback Church in a sense reclaimed the Twelve Steps for Christianity in their now global program Celebrate Recovery (CR). They expanded the steps to again include all forms of human woundedness: hurts, habits, and hang-ups. Hurts cover past physical, sexual, or emotional abuse and family dysfunction (i.e., wounds). Habits refer to addictions, such as drugs, alcohol, sex, gambling, food, or anything else we idolize. Hang-ups refer to negative mental attitudes, like anxiety, depression, or low self-esteem. Essentially, it means anything that causes shame, guilt, despair, depression, anger, or pain.

CR helps us acknowledge that every human being is in recovery from sin. We all have lost our Garden of Eden. We all know the gift of desperation in some way. Not all of us suffer from the diseases that show up as addictions, but each of us has a broken condition that manifests in the various ways we try to fill the hole in our being with the temporary balms of food, sex, work, control, approval, and other banes.

The steps are not a series of boxes to be checked, after which one is suddenly "cured." One does not graduate this program. These steps are a lifelong journey of spiritual growth. They keep us in touch with our "thorns" and give us a way to remain in communion with our wounded healer. The steps are a "design for living" and a process of yielding our weaknesses to God, where we find the perfect power of grace.

These substitutions for God's presence are the symptoms of an underlying disease. As a missionary pastor, I'm often brought face to face with the depths of brokenness and the need for grace. Every time I watch a couple divorce for marital unfaithfulness, witness the desperation of a person who seemingly can't stop drinking, hear the confession of a longtime Christian hooked on pornography, or work with parents who abandoned their children in the midst of their drug use, I see this need for grace.

In many instances, I have seen God work in miraculous and reconciling ways.

In a post-Christian society, discussions about "sin" and the "cross" can shut down acknowledgment of grace. Bad Christians happen to good people, and "bad theology" runs rampant around us. The damage is apparent when helping an individual recognize God's reconciling love. Some Christians and seekers struggle with the concept of God's redemption through "sacrifice." By analogy, Martin Luther King, Jr. reminds us that "violence merely increases hate. . . . Darkness cannot drive out darkness, only light can do that."[7]

Historically, four primary models of atonement explain how Jesus's sacrifice reconciles us to God. The *Christus victor* model emphasizes a cosmic battle taking place between good and evil on the cross. This model holds that through the crucifixion and resurrection of Jesus, the powers of death and evil binding humanity were ultimately defeated. The *moral example* model describes Jesus's death as an example of God's self-sacrificial love, which inspires humanity to love accordingly. The *satisfaction* model maintains that sin was an affront to God's justice. Hence, Jesus stepped in as a substitute on behalf of sin-ridden humanity. The *penal-substitutionary* model highlights that God imputed the guilt of our sins onto Jesus, and Jesus received our punishment in our stead.[8]

Each of these models has strengths and weaknesses, yet with unintended consequences contribute to an ideology of violence. One way to reframe this dilemma is captured powerfully by Dan Bell: "God does not demand blood ... we do."[9] Jesus is the fullness of God's beauty, truth, and goodness—enfleshed. The life of heaven comes to earth, not simply as a satisfaction or substitution but as God's pure, nonviolent, unbounded love—and we give him hell. Thomas Aquinas said, "the greatest offence

---

7. *Where Do We Go from Here?* (Boston: Beacon, 1967), 67.

8. Shirley C. Guthrie, *Christian Doctrine* (Louisville, KY: Westminster John Knox, 1994), 252–60.

9. See Dan Bell in D. B. Laytham, *God Does Not Entertain, Play "Matchmaker," Hurry, Demand Blood, Cure Every Illness* (Grand Rapids, MI: Brazos, 2009), 58.

was perpetrated in the passion of Christ, since his slayers committed the most grievous of sins."[10] Jesus's death ends all need for violence. The cross is ultimately a way God engages our sin and suffering. Charles Wesley proclaims, "God for me hath died: my Lord, my love, is crucified!"[11] As S. Mark Heim states, "Redemptive violence is our equation. Jesus didn't volunteer to get into God's justice machine. God volunteered to get into ours. God used our own sin to save us."[12]

Jürgen Moltmann helps navigate this by centering our understanding of atonement in the Trinity. He discusses the cross not only in a soteriological sense, but from a Trinitarian framework we are reminded that Jesus the Son is also God. The crucified Christ is the "crucified God," not simply a moment of transaction between the two.[13] Furthermore, it is not only the cross that is redemptive, all of Jesus's life and death are imperative for our redemption. Saint Athanasius articulates, "God became like us [human] so that we might become like God."[14] The resurrection demonstrates the completed work of redemption and total atonement (Rom 1:4). Christ's atonement is not the entirety of Christ's work; it's the foundation for his present work as the Risen Lord. Hence, God's grace transforms our lives through a personal relationship with Jesus and the infilling of the Holy Spirit.

Every generation seems to manifest a distinct form of sin-bentness. The pervading struggle of our time is shame: a painful feeling of humiliation or distress caused by a conscious sense of not-enough-ness. Shame is a self-worth issue, in which we question the value of our own personhood.

---

10. Aquinas in *Documents of the Christian Church* (Oxford: Oxford University Press, 1999), 161.

11. "O Love Divine, What Hast Thou Done," no. 287, *The United Methodist Hymnal*, stanza 4.

12. *Saved from Sacrifice: A Theology of the Cross* (Grand Rapids, MI: Eerdmans, 2006), xi.

13. *The Crucified God: The Cross of Christ as the Foundation and Criticism of Christian Theology.* (Minneapolis: Fortress, 1993), 201–02.

14. Athanasius, *On the Incarnation* (Crestwood, NY: St. Vladimir's Seminary Press, 1993), 55.

When young people share openly about their struggles in fresh expressions of church, the conversation usually leans toward shame. In the super-competitive nature of a consumerist society, where the "winners" are idolized, the rest of us are the losers. Those of us who don't possess super-model beauty, immense wealth, or genius intelligence, can develop a mentality of deficiency. The network society floods us with global images of success and wealth, perfectly filtered and Instagram-worthy. This is a breeding ground for shame.

Perhaps we need a new theory of reconciliation for the network society, the *Jesus Antivirus Model*. Think of it as a "divine defrag" of the virus-infected hard drive of the universe. Sin causes fragmentation at every level of creation: fragmentation in our relationships with God, each other, and to creation itself. This breech leads us to acknowledge in our hyper-individualism that something is lacking. Shame pushes us into isolation. Jesus incarnates himself in the virus-ridden network, in a specific "node" called Nazareth (space of place). Like anti-virus software, Jesus draws the virus infecting the system into one location, concentrated in his own body on the cross. "He carried in his own body on the cross the sins we committed. He did this so that we might live in righteousness, having nothing to do with sin. By his wounds you were healed (1 Pet 2:24).

The "rulers and authorities" gather collectively at the cross and are "disarmed" and triumphed over in a public spectacle (Col 2:15). All the forces of moral and natural evil—imperial evil, religious evil, demonic evil—converge literally in an earthquake in one place, in one moment in time (Matt 27:51). There, concentrated in the pain-wracked body of Jesus himself, with the virus of sin isolated in his own flesh (2 Cor 5:21), he takes on "our shame" in himself (Heb 12:2), and destroys its power through his own sacrificial death (1 Cor 15:55-56). Through the resurrection, ascension, and sending of the Spirit, every Christian becomes a microcosm of Jesus, a cell in the larger body. We become the anti-virus, spreading reconciliation in the space of flows throughout the whole system

(2 Cor 5:18), until Jesus returns to bring the new creation in all its fullness (Matt 24:30, Rev 21–22).

In fresh expressions of church, as relationships are formed, some toxic theology about the human condition is encountered. Many people get hung up on "divine child abuse" theology: they hear that God the Father is punishing the hell out of his Son for our mistakes. A Wesleyan-Arminian understanding of restoration, the sacred worth and great value of every person, is refreshing to emerging generations. We emphasize the remarkable depth of God's love, to enter into the living hell we can inflict upon each other, to end the animal and grain sacrificial system and the need for violence once and for all. God descends into the deepest recesses of our human brokenness to show us who we really are, to heal our shame. This is indeed "good news" for most people.

The fresh expressions movement can be applied as a remix of the early Wesleyan discipleship system. Once again, the "glad tidings of salvation" are being "proclaimed in the highways" and the fields. Now those fields and highways have taken the form of the "nodes" and "flows" of the network society.

People connect over hobbies, passions, and practices, across geographic barriers. Planting fresh expressions amid communities gathered around these practices involves an incarnational approach that ultimately transforms the practices themselves. The pioneers lead the group to begin intentionally exploring the Christian faith. This includes a mixture of both formal learning (intentional conversations) and social learning (simply sharing in the rhythms of life together). More mature believers may begin to form mentorships with younger apprentices, spending time outside the group, discipling them through the messy relational process.

Fresh Expressions is not about simply gathering in cool spaces to "play church." Very real disciples are being formed in these very real microchurches, in much the same way as the early Methodist movement. In our local churches, we are experimenting with Wesley's model of societies, classes, and bands. We identify each one of our fresh expressions in one of those stages. Each of our fresh expressions is overseen by a pioneer, the "ordinary" Christian from among the "priesthood of all believers."

So, for instance, at Tattoo Parlor Church, Higher Power Hour (church in the chemical dependency unit of the local rehab), and Paws of Praise (church in a dog park), God's prevenient grace is at work as we are creating a community of belonging with so called "nones" and "dones" and believing unfolds at the pace of grace (society). In Burritos and Bibles (church in a Tijuana Flats), Family Table Community Dinner, and Yoga Church, God's justifying grace is at work as people open to Christianity, engage scripture, feel free to publicly pray, or take communion for the first time, and share about "how goes it with their soul" (class). At Women, Wine, and the Word, a group of women gather in Francesco's Ristorante for the purposes of studying scripture, growing in sanctification, and brainstorming mission opportunities in the community (band).[15]

While these contextual expressions may not be exacting illustrations of the early Wesleyan system, we can see how they reflect a Methodism that's remerging powerfully through the fresh expressions movement.

In these gatherings, we've seen all kinds of beautiful grace moments unfold in people's lives along the journey as they are healed of their shame. When a young woman wept and said, "I slept with some guy Friday night and I don't even remember his name," the band of women enfolded her in love, and said things like, "We understand, we love you, and we are with you." When's the last time something like that confession happened in a Sunday morning worship gathering? But isn't that the very place where it should be happening? We've seen people go from praying publicly for the first time to leading their own fresh expression within a year's time. We've seen people convicted of their cursing, their smoking, their overeating, and be healed of their "isms."

I'm utterly convinced that fresh expressions, by creating places where folks can make the journey of grace and uncover the masterpiece beneath

---

15. See https Michael Beck and Walter Edwards: //freshexpressionsus.org/2018/03/05/history-repeating-discipleship/.

the mess, is making disciples in ways we have largely failed to do in the inherited church for decades.

Field Story—
Dr. Dwight Zscheile
Vice President of Innovation and
Professor of Congregational Mission and Leadership
Luther Seminary, St. Paul, Minnesota
More Stories from The Episcopal Church

Lightwave Red Lodge, Rural Suffolk, UK

Red Lodge is a growing village in the east of England with new housing developments. Families moving into the area are typically disconnected from each other and community. The Lightwave ministry utilizes a local community sports pavilion and offers multiple ways for various people in the neighborhood to connect and be nourished holistically. This includes young adult board games once a month, Friday night youth cafes, socials for single ladies, men's breakfasts, toddlers and parents sessions, messy church, café church, and breakfast chat (primarily for seniors). These gatherings forefront being together, cultivating relationships, and sharing food or simple refreshments. They also typically include some kind of spiritual component—discussions on spiritual topics, building Bible stories out of Legos (for children and youth), short sharing of faith stories with invitation for conversation at tables, simple prayer practices. A food bank and resume and interview counseling are provided regularly, funded by the local town council.

Tubestation, Polzeath, UK

Tubestation is a Christian community on the coast in the west of England that focuses on the surfing, skateboarding, and arts communities. They have a café, art gallery, and halfpipe skate ramp. The café, gallery, and halfpipe are open throughout the week. Sundays there is a focused church gathering in the café that is highly participatory, with scripture, songs, storytelling, discussion, and sometimes dance and spoken word. The space and worship reflect the ethos of coastal skate/surf/environmental culture.

Curry and Questions, Northampton, UK

A group of men in a suburban area meet monthly in a local Indian restaurant for discussion around faith. The group is mostly non-Christian and everyone is invited to come as they are and share whatever they want to about spirituality, God, meaning, life after death, why bad things happen to good people, etc. It is facilitated by a local priest.

The Peace Project, Ipswich, UK

A weekly play and social time for children age 0-5 and parents called Baby Steps is accompanied by a final ten-minute time of meditation in a community space run by a local church. Lights are dimmed, sparkly lights on the ceiling are turned on, bean bags and carpets come out, and a guided meditation invites participants into a time of prayer, stillness, and peace. The children and parents are reluctant to get up and leave!

Thirst Café Church, Cambridge, UK

A few parents who were Christian noticed that other parents wanted to connect and talk after dropping their kids off at school. They got permission to use the teacher lounge to offer coffee, fruit, and juice to parents who wanted to stay and hang out after school started. Over time, they added an optional time of spiritual reflection/prayer at the end. They invited anyone who wanted to stay to spend fifteen minutes in prayer, with a lit candle. They asked if they could share a brief story from the life of Jesus ("one of the world's great spiritual teachers") and have conversation about it. Over time, this grew into a community of people exploring Christian faith.

Forest Church, Multiple Locations

Recognizing that many people experience the sacred outdoors, Forest Church involves gathering people in nature for simple prayers, scripture readings, conversation, and reflection. Sometimes, this can take the form of walks/hikes with a spiritual focus. One example is Worship in the Wild in north Wales. They take a different circular walk each month. The walk is divided into sections, where they pause and ponder, with silence, prayer, a reflection question or discussion prompt. For example, after walking through a dense thicket of brush and trees, the group might gather, pause, and reflect on times in their lives when they passed through a difficult stretch in their lives and how they grew spiritually during that season.

Missional Field Kit:
Mapping Milestones on the Journey of Grace

With your team, discuss the journey of grace. Look at how John Wesley organized the societies, classes, and bands, corresponding with "waves of grace"—prevenient, justifying, and sanctifying.

Here are some questions to consider together:

1. How is the Holy Spirit "making disciples of Jesus Christ" in our church? How are we collaborating?

2. What is the "sin-bentness" pervading our community? (for example, shame, guilt, racism, addiction, and so on) How do we know this?

3. Where are we creating space or gatherings for people in the "prevenient grace" leg of their journey—those who may not be Christian yet?

4. Where are we creating space or gatherings for people in the "justifying grace" leg of their journey—those accepting Christ, and working out the implications for their lives?

5. Where are we creating space or gatherings for people in the "sanctifying grace" leg of their journey—those seeking to "love God and neighbor with all their heart, soul, mind, and body"?

6. How many people in our congregation are involved in ministry —leading, serving, and volunteering?

7. How many "pioneers" are actively seeking to form community with people outside the church?

You may find it helpful to draw out your responses on a whiteboard, to map out the milestones on the journey of grace.

DOWNLOAD 6

Jesus and the New Pantheon

Orthodoxy is complicated. Earlier we explored the fact that Ethiopia is home to one of the oldest continuous churches in the world. The Ethiopian Orthodox Church belongs to a connection called the Oriental Orthodox Churches.

While the Oriental Orthodox shared in full communion with the Imperial Roman Church for a period, at the Council of Chalcedon in 451 CE they parted ways. The point of separation was primarily a difference of Christology. Oriental Orthodoxy rejected the Chalcedonian definition of Jesus' nature as "hypostatic union." Hypostasis refers to the mysterious joining of Jesus' two complete natures, both fully human and fully divine, in one *person*.

The Oriental Orthodox claims to be holding to an earlier miaphysite formula (Greek μία (mía, "one") and φύσις (*phúsis*, in this case "nature")), or that Jesus is fully divine and fully human, united in one *nature* (*physis*). Early Oriental Orthodox prelates were concerned that the Chalcedonian definition implied a possible repudiation of the Trinity or a concession to Nestorianism, which was condemned as heresy at the Council of Ephesus in 431 CE.

While to some inhabitants of the western Church this may seem like a matter of theological hair splitting or mere semantics, this is not the case for adherents of the Eastern Orthodox Church. The adjective *Oriental* is synonymous with the adjective *Eastern*, meaning there is no real distinction between the terms. Nevertheless, these are two distinct bodies of Christians, who while sharing some beliefs, remain divided over the mysterious mechanics of Christology.

The Eastern Orthodox Church considers itself the oldest Church in Christendom. It is the second largest body of Christians with 225 million people worldwide (yet less than six million in North America). The Eastern Orthodox describe Oriental Orthodox as a connection of false churches, outside the historic faith.[1]

While many consider Oriental Orthodox as broadly part of the trinitarian Nicene Christianity shared by today's mainstream churches (indeed maybe even one of its oldest branches), two ancient and major expressions of the Christian faith do not agree on an essential aspect of dogma.

In the eleventh century another split occurred in the Church between the Orthodox East and Latin West. The "Great Schism" of 1054 represented a formal separation between Rome and Orthodoxy based on two areas of disagreement: the role of the papacy, and the manner in which doctrine is to be interpreted.

Are the millions of Christians, many faithful adherents who live a life of holy love for God and neighbor, actually less than "true" Christians based on these historic doctrinal disputes? There has never been a single "orthodox theology" in history. Tracing back even to the four Gospels we see distinct theologies that reflect the writers/communities' contextual circumstances.

Justo L. González was the first to outline "three types of theology" generally considered to be orthodox expressions of the Christian faith, each tracing back to the earliest centuries of the church.[2] Dorothee Sölle

---

1. *The Non-Chalcedonian Heretics*, 41.

2. González, *Christian Thought Revisited*

described these types as 1. orthodox/conservative 2. liberal 3. radical/liberation theology.[3] Roman Catholic missiologists Bevans and Schroeder outline these three paradigms of theology as Type A. Tertullian in Rome, conservative, emphasizing law. Type B. Origen in Alexandria, liberal, emphasizing truth. Type C. Irenaeus representing Antioch, liberation, emphasizing history.[4]

Let's examine these theological streams and their origins briefly.

Irenaeus was born in Smyrna in the region of Asia Minor. Antioch was the principal city of the area and the place where Christianity was first recognized as a distinct religion in its own rite (Acts 11:25-26). Ignatius served as bishop of Antioch in the formative years of the church, and Polycarp served as Bishop of nearby Smyrna in the same region. Scholars believe that Matthew, John, Revelation, and many of Paul's letters were a product of the early Christian communities there. Irenaeus was deeply influenced by these leaders, and through Polycarp, who was likely a direct disciple of John, was one generation removed from the first apostles. He migrated to the Roman frontier city of Lyons in Gaul but brought a distinct Antiochian theology with him.

Tertullian was born in Carthage, (approximately 155–160 CE) a cultural and educational center second only to Rome. He was educated in grammar, rhetoric, literature, philosophy, and law. Little is known of his early life. Tertullian completed his education in Carthage, the traveled to Rome, likely to begin work as a lawyer. Tertullian became a leading voice of the African church, offering instruction for believers and writing as an Apologist defending Christian beliefs and practices. His prolific writings defending the faith included treatises on theological problems against specific opponents: "Against Marcion," "Against Hermogenes," "Against Valentinus," and "Concerning the Resurrection of the Flesh". He also penned the first Christian works on baptism, a Christian doctrine of humanity, as

---

3. Sölle, *Thinking about God*

4. Bevans and Schroeder, *Constants in Context*, 2004.

well as essays on prayer and devotion, and the treatise directed against all heresy, "Concerning the Prescription of Heretics."

Origen (185–254 CE) likely born in Alexandria, is considered the most important theologian and biblical scholar of the early Greek church. Origen was a pupil of Clement of Alexandria, whom he succeeded as head of the Catechetical school under the authority of the bishop Demetrius. He was impacted by Neoplatonist philosophy. Origen learned Hebrew and began to compile his masterwork *Hexapla*, a synopsis of Old Testament versions: the Hebrew and the Septuagint (an authoritative Greek version of the Old Testament). He also wrote extensive exegetical works including commentaries, homilies, and scholia (reflections on particular passages or books).

Unlike Tertullian, Irenaeus was not a brilliant lawyer. Unlike Origen, he was also not a keen academic. He was the pastor of a Christian outpost in a frontier town, and his theology bears the mark of a practical theologian who was engaged in ministry as a practitioner and an apologist. In fact, he warned against criticism of the "simplicity of the holy presbyters" and "how much better a simple religious man is than a blasphemous and impudent sophist"[5] (Sophist: paid teacher of philosophy and rhetoric in ancient Greece).

González suggests that Type C is the oldest stream of Christian theology, closer to the original witnesses collected in the New Testament and influenced by the sub-apostolic tradition. Whereas Tertullian and Origen were deeply immersed in Hellenistic culture, rooted in Platonic philosophy and Roman law, Irenaeus produced a theology that was both less legalistic and less abstract.

We can likely locate our theological traditions in one of these ancient streams. In reality, all theology is "conjunctive theology," which often holds differing thoughts together in creative tension. For instance, as we have seen, Jesus is both "fully human" and "fully God." There are dimensions of Jesus's realm "already here" and "not yet." God is a "seeking" and

---

5. Irenaeus, *Against Heresies*, V. 20:2

"sending" God. We believe in "prevenient" and "justifying" and "sanctifying" grace. Ministers have preached in "pulpits" and "fields." A God-shaped church is both "missional" and "attractional." The list goes on.

In terms of interacting with persons of other religions, we must hold together "openness and conviction" in creative tension.[6]

I meet weekly with a group of folks in church basements and classrooms from various religious beliefs (Buddhists, Muslims, Hindus, and more). While most are not Christians, they meet for the same reason many people meet on Sunday mornings—they yearn to be closer with God, they desire the fellowship of other human beings, and some just want to stay sober. I once wondered why these folks met so faithfully on the church property throughout the week, but wouldn't darken the door of a church on Sunday morning. I have always seen the church as a place of hope and healing, but many others do not share my sentiments. In the case of the anonymous fellowship to which I belong, although these folks may not proclaim faith in Jesus Christ, the Holy Spirit is active and alive in them and empowering them to live a different kind of life—one free of drugs and alcohol.

Early Christians emphasized a personal experience of God as a loving being who relentlessly seeks and desires to be in relationship with all (Luke 15). We urgently desire that all humanity come to know the God revealed in Jesus Christ. That desire drove pioneers out to the fields, and that desire has driven us into our communities ever since. We are sent with hearts aflame with God's love, to give our lives to God's grand search and recovery effort, *and* simultaneously in radical openness we are aware that God is working in the people already before we get there.

Particularly an understanding of prevenient grace—*the grace that goes before us*—is drawing all humanity into a relationship is helpful here. This understanding should shape our interactions with people from other Christian traditions and religions, as well as "nones and dones." Søren

6. Theodore Runyon, *The New Creation: John Wesley's Theology Today* (Nashville: Abingdon, 1998), 215.

Kierkegaard said, "Christ is the Truth inasmuch as he is the way. [One] who does not follow the way also abandons the truth. We possess Christ's truth only by imitating him, not by speculating about him."[7] God the Son, as "the way," came to heal the brokenness of humanity, not just a single people group. Christ continually reaches out to the marginalized (Matt 15:21-28), those considered racially or religiously impure (John 4), and the religious other excluded from the community (Luke 7). God the Spirit continues to push those bounds and "go native" (Acts 2:8), operating in the world through all the diverse people God the Father has created (Acts 11:12). The very diversity of the peoples of the earth is a reflection of the diverse singularity of the Trinity (Gen 1:27).

This "conjunctive theology" put on flesh for me while working in Guatemala among indigenous religions. I went convicted to offer Christ. What I discovered was Christ had "gone native" before me. In the midst of institutionalized poverty, I saw *agape* [love]. My mind was opened to recognize that the Holy Spirit was already working. My heart was opened to the shamefulness of proclaiming a highly personalized, spiritualized, Western message of salvation with no contextual specificity.[8] I want all people to accept Christ, but whether they do or not—I must accept them. That experience shaped my missional mindset in the pioneering of fresh expressions.

Gil Rendle noted that the church was planted in an "aberrant time." This refers to a non-repeatable amalgamation of conditions to form a particular historical moment.[9] The twentieth-century conditions that enabled the thriving of a Christendom model for the church are no more. We are jungle people who must now learn to live in a desert. The ecosystem

---

7.   Søren Kierkegaard, *Training in Christianity*, quoted in Michael Frost and Alan Hirsch, *ReJesus: A Wild Messiah for a Missional Church* (Peabody, MA: Hendrickson, 2009), 53.

8.   E. Tamez, *The Amnesty of Grace: Justification by Faith from a Latin American Perspective* (1993), 21.

9.   Gilbert R. Rendle, *Quietly Courageous: Leading the Church in a Changing World* (Lanham, MD: Rowman & Littlefield, 2019), 21–23.

has changed, and our relationship with the environment is part of the challenge to live in a new world.

Following Christ's incarnational model, we must "go native," enter the world of the other, love them, and pursue the relational opportunities that naturally unfold. At the church I serve, more come to Christ in church parking lots and basements, tattoo parlors, restaurants, and dog parks, throughout the week than in the sanctuary. Fresh expressions are stocked ponds for "people fishing" (Matt 4:19). And so, with deep conviction *and* total openness, I seek to take John Wesley's statement to heart: "Though we may not think alike, may we not all love alike?"[10]

Time for a Remix

In the United States, at least two generations have grown up in a rapidly secularizing and pluralistic culture. Today, emerging generations are growing up with a predominantly minimal experience of church. For a few more years, the majority in attendance at most congregations are "the builders," those born before 1946, who endured the Great Depression and World War II. The inevitable departure of these saints into the rest of God, and the convergence of other forces, was described by Lovett Weems as a "death tsunami," which statistically crested in 2018. This analogy can easily apply to churches across the theological and denominational spectrum.[11]

The era of "Blue Laws," those restrictions designed to ban Sunday activities to promote the observance of a day of Sabbath, is over. The age of Christendom, which was governed by white Christian Protestants, is past; the age of the new pantheon has come. The Roman pantheon described the constituency of all the gods collectively; it included the noteworthy gods of subjugated peoples. There are multiple similarities between

10. John Wesley, *The Standard Sermons in Modern English*, ed. K. C. Kinghorn (Nashville, 2002), 102.

11. Lovett H. Weems, *Focus: The Real Challenges That Face The United Methodist Church* (Nashville: Abingdon Press, 2011), 2.

ancient paganism and contemporary relativism.[12] The new US religious landscape is of the potluck variety. All religious paths are equally valid and meaningful, just take a sample of each if you like, and save room for dessert! This is called "personal religion" by sociologists. In the new pantheon for personal religion, all the "gods" share the same mythical space. Which "god" or combinations of "gods" one chooses is more a matter of personal preference than a matter of ultimate significance. Which "god" works best for you? Spirituality for personal religion is privatized and marketed to consumers like all other aspects of life.

In personal religion, each of the many "gods" has a devoted tribe. What Jesus called mammon, or money, is the true Zeus—king of the gods—in the theism of consumerist society. Len Sweet writes, "The market has become a god and consumption a religion. . . . The empire of goods has become the empire of our gods."[13]

Emerging generations hyper-connected by digital flows are rarely sold out to a single "tribe." They push against institutional iterations of religion that seem hypocritical and archaic. They also rarely commit to a single organization. As noted earlier, this doesn't mean they won't participate in an organization; it means they want to enjoy the freedom of participating in several organizations whose values and interests align with their own.

Therefore, one default spiritual mode in the US is agnostic. Some educational systems train us to be skeptical and to apply critical thinking concerning every truth claim. Regrettably, some educated persons think their reason is superior, which can make them arrogant toward the other, unable to critique, for example, a scientific world view in tension with a-religious faith.

While there is a profound spiritual openness in our culture, one of the fastest growing tribes is *none*—those who indicate no religious affiliation. While the language may be moving away from religiosity and

12.   David Goodhew, Andrew Roberts, and Michael Volland, *Fresh!: An Introduction to Fresh Expressions of Church and Pioneer Ministry* (London, UK: SCM Press, 2012), 4–5.

13.   Leonard I. Sweet, *Me and We: God's New Social Gospel* (Nashville: Abingdon Press, 2014), 99–101.

toward all-inclusive spirituality, religion is very much alive in the US. For example, consider a religious devotion to sports: the gladiatorial games of the new Rome. Consider "the largest religious revival you know nothing about." Heather Smith coined the term "Athletica" as she playfully, satirically but with compelling obviousness, noted how by every metric, youth sports leagues have all the major characteristics of a religion. There is liturgy, multiple weekly meetings, rituals, behavioral covenants, sacrifices, uniforms, worship gatherings, and membership fees. In fact, families demonstrate incredible devotion to sports in an unprecedented way. One could question if the American church in the twentieth century ever engaged and claimed people's whole lives this way.[14] On any given Sunday, many families welcome Lady Athletica to the US pantheon!

The New Testament emerged in a pantheistic environment. Paul's proclamation of the gospel and the early church spread in this type of culture. In the Book of Acts we see faith communities quick on their feet and highly responsive. Christian theology and the structures of the church were taking shape as they emerged in the process of mission through engaging the contextual realities.

For instance:

Acts 6:1-7. Leadership was applied and improvised from a missional imperative.

Acts 11:1-18. The Spirit guided the church to abolish long held convictions that divided people along racial and religious lines—to "make no distinction between them and us" (11:12).

Acts 15. The church "gathered" (Jerusalem, inherited) and "scattered" (Antioch, a fresh expression of church). They cooperated, conferenced, and made major adjustments for the sake of the greater mission (15:28-29).

---

14.   Heather Smith, "Inside America's Largest Religious Revival You Know Nothing About," *The Federalist,* November 2017, http://thefederalist.com/2017/11/10/inside-americas-largest-religious-revival-know-nothing/, accessed November 2017.

Acts 16. Context determined Paul's missional approach. At Philippi, there were no synagogues, so Paul found "a place of prayer" down by the river. A fresh expression of church was born in Lydia's home.

Acts 17:1-9. The disciples disturbed the imperial peace, rather than cooperated with it, and engaged in non-violent subversion (17:7).

Acts 17:16-34. Paul adjusted to context. A true innovator, he used cultural phenomenon as a medium of proclamation (17:22-24).

Let's consider Paul's experience in Athens at the Areopagus.

While Paul was waiting for them in Athens, he was deeply distressed to see that the city was full of idols (Acts 17:16 ESV).

First, Paul had the uncanny ability to pay attention to a context, to see both the fragmentation and the possibilities. Do we see our own contexts in this way? Listening, paying attention, looking for the sore spots in our community with soft eyes is crucial in healthy missional engagement. Next, he was "distressed," meaning his heart was troubled by the condition of the city. Do we care enough about our own zip code to be distressed over the fragmentation? Genuine care for our community, a healthy love for the people in it, is the starting point of every vital fresh expression of church.

Paul traveled to a third place, a space that served as the center of their curiosity.

All Athenians as well as the foreigners who live in Athens used to spend their time doing nothing but talking about or listening to the newest thing. Paul stood up in the middle of the council on Mars Hill and said, "People of Athens, I see that you are very religious in every way." (Acts 17:21-22)

Athens was the cradle of Greek civilization and a place that valued education. There were two major schools of thought—the Stoics and the

Epicureans. In Paul's day, the Areopagus had become a forum for the exchange of free-flowing ideas between Epicureans, Stoics, and other philosophers. Paul was advantaged in having an extensive education among the Pharisees. He was highly competent in the skill of *translation*: the ability to build a bridge of meaning between culture and the gospel. Paul paid attention, analyzed culture, and started by affirming the life-giving tendencies already present in the culture: "I see that you are very religious in every way." He started by constructing the bridge of meaning on their side of the shore.

He continued in the Areopagus Address:

> As I was walking through town and carefully observing your objects of worship, I even found an altar with this inscription: "To an unknown God." What you worship as unknown, I now proclaim to you. (Acts 17:22-23)

In his message, he used the inscriptions on their own temples as a medium for his proclamation. He did his homework and integrated what he had to say with their locality in a contextually appropriate way. He quoted their own poets and philosophers; he used their own soundtracks on the Billboard Hot 100 Chart and their own New York Times Best Sellers lists. He respected the people enough to immerse himself in their context and thinking. He acknowledged what was good, beautiful, and true in their culture. He even nodded toward their pantheistic conceptions, but then unabashedly lifted the truth of Jesus.

In the network society, the web as a global integrated communication system is (on some nodes in social networks) the new Aeropagus. Manuel Castells notes that the culture of real virtuality

> weakens considerably the symbolic power of traditional senders external to the system, transmitting through historically encoded social habits: religion, morality, authority, traditional values, political ideology . . . unless they *recode* themselves in the new system, where the power becomes

multiplied by the electronic materialization of the spiritually transmitted habits (italics mine).[15]

Paul and his missionary teams were *recoding* themselves, programming the truth of Jesus into the Greco-Roman system. Pioneers of incarnational mission in the Great Awakenings recoded the Christian faith into the dawning industrial society, in "plain words for plain people" by harnessing the emerging technologies. This is what fresh expressions pioneers are up to today.

In an age when the space of flows and the space of places coexist and interconnect, and a presence in the digital landscape makes a physical building unnecessary for the encounter, pioneers are harnessing social media and networking technologies to create Jesus communities in and among those larger networks. People are connecting and meeting in communal spaces in new relational arrangements that look like the church in Acts, "recoding" Christian truth into the system. We can be an incarnate presence on the digital frontier, harnessing these technologies that have become the means through which fresh expressions of church are organized, promoted, and sustained. By creating "disruptive innovation departments" in local churches, we can bypass the traditional ways that churches once solely relied upon to engage the community.

In social media flows, we connect with those outside typical church circles. Just as technology has become an extension of the human mind, so it is becoming an extension of the human communities of faith. Emerging generations who get their news through social media will also have their first encounters with churches through social media.

Most fresh expressions create free pages to describe basic info and location times that can be shared throughout an extensive relational network. Events can be created, friends invite friends. A relational cascade can stretch out far and wide across the digital landscape. People outside one person's relational network may be reached through another. Some fresh

---

15. Manuel Castells, *The Rise of the Network Society* (Oxford and Malden, MA: Blackwell, 2000), 406.

expressions use meetup.com or other similar platforms to create groups and invite new people. The hyper-connectivity that the internet provides can be harnessed to build actual communities in real first, second, third, and digital places.

The inherited congregation may have the traditional centralized platform with websites and social media pages, like nodes and hubs within the network. But the fresh expressions serve as a decentralized "network" of relational transactions. Any person who can use social media can start a new fresh expression, organize a movement, or share a message. Wise churches will harness this capacity rather than attack it. While it challenges denominational systems, professional clergy, dedicated facilities, and traditional communication channels, if embraced or permitted, it could release the next remixed iteration of the church.

Churches have been largely focused on competing for the dwindling population of "already Christians" while blinded to the larger reality of the new pluralistic culture. Fresh expressions are about cultivating churches in the "fields" with this growing demographic of "nones and dones." It's about forming relationships with the spiritually open in the places where they do life. This is how Christianity spread like a virus through the Greco-Roman colonizing networks, and it is how the Evangelical Revival spread across the seas.

Field Story
Good Neighbor Home Church @ The Jennings House
Lori Jennings, Laity
Vice President, American Baptist Churches of PA and DE
GraceCrossing Community Church
Phoenixville, Pennsylvania (a suburb of Philadelphia).

In the fall of 2022, we started a weekly gathering on Tuesday nights in my home. I'd call it a hybrid of Home Church and Dinner Church. It started off small with four church leaders and grew to fifteen people give or take, with guests now and then. Those attending range from age 13 to 65. We start off with a meal together promptly at 6:30 p.m. Sometimes the meal is supplied by the host, sometimes its byog (bring your own grub). But we sit around the tables, discussing our past week, and usually sharing laughs but sometimes a few tears. At 7 p.m., usually as few more straggle in, we begin our discussion. We start by asking, where did you see Jesus in the past week in your life? After sharing, we read a Jesus story, straight out of the Bible. We take turns reading the same passage four times, using different Bible versions, then there's discussion on the passage after each reading. What stood out to you? Did you learn something different? How does it apply in your life? It's amazing how many times you might have heard a Bible story and somehow never realized this part or that. Hearing what others have gleaned in the same passage also opens opportunity for new learning and understanding.

Those who come to are a mix of people from all ages and backgrounds: A couple who are fed up with church and church people, who found friends and comfort in a safe environment. A twenty-something young adult who grew up in church but doesn't attend much anymore. A former pastor and his wife who experienced the dark side of church folks. We've got some teenagers looking for a place to ask questions and participate in open discussion. A mom, who gives a lot on Sundays at the traditional worship service and needs to have a space to talk about Jesus and explore the Bible. Some newer believers, who don't know much about the Bible and want to learn more. And then there are a few who come for the fellowship and friendship but put up with the Bible discussion. We finish promptly at 8 p.m., as most have work or school the next day. This works for those in the group who want to attend but like a hard stop/end.

Home church is real, messy, not scripted, and very casual. Come as you are, Jesus will meet you there, and he'll bring friends. We come with our baggage, praises, or struggles to share. We get closer to Jesus and each other.

Missional Field Kit:
Recoding Exercises—
Finding Good News in the Culture

This is an exercise in interpreting culture. Gather your fresh expressions team together and play one or each of the following YouTube clips.

- *The Lion King* clip: https://youtu.be/yGQnGQzlAm

- "This Is Me": https://youtu.be/XLFEvHWD_NE

- Ikea Commercial, "Start Something New":
  https://youtu.be/lQwrpmUmVeo

- Perhaps you have another movie clip, song, commercial, or cultural piece that would be more appropriate for your context. The main idea here is to find the "good news" in the culture and how to use it as a bridge to the truth of Jesus.

Simply watch, and then ask yourself these three questions:

1. What touched you about this clip?

2. Where did you see the gospel?

3. How would you use this piece as a medium to tell someone about God?

A God of *Withness* in a World of Hurt

Thomas Helwys would not be the last Baptist to be imprisoned and ultimately die for his convictions. For Baptists the commitment to personal autonomy lived out under the Lordship of Jesus, coupled with the conviction that Christian's ought to be free from coercion by corrupt governments has continued to be a struggle. In these commitments there is a tension between the reign of God and the suffering and often systemic evil so prevalent in the world. There is no greater example of the embodiment of these values than a Baptist minister named Dr. Martin Luther King Jr. King served as pastor of Dexter Avenue King Baptist Church in Montgomery, Alabama, when he began his Civil Rights activism.

As a black child growing up in the south of a segregated United States, he experienced discrimination and abuse. King pursued and achieved the highest level of education possible. A brilliant student, he skipped several grades and graduated early. He started at Morehouse College at just fifteen years old, where he earned a Bachelor of Arts. He earned a Master of Divinity from Crozer Theological Seminary, then finally a doctorate in systematic theology from Boston University in 1955, at the age of just twenty-six.

On December 1, 1955, Rosa Parks, another African American, was arrested for violating segregation laws when she rejected a bus driver's order to vacate her seat for a white passenger in Montgomery, Alabama. Parks was frustrated with heightened discrimination and the regular, legal, public lynchings of innocent black persons. In the wake of this event, King was asked to provide leadership and he indeed arose to the occasion.

As the newly elected leader of the Montgomery Improvement Association (MIA), he coordinated the Montgomery bus boycott, a thirteen-month mass protest. In the struggle for civil rights, King was arrested numerous times. On February 21, 1956, a Montgomery grand jury indicted King and other MIA leaders for violating the anti-boycott law. King was found guilty and sentenced to a $500 fine or 386 days in jail. The case was appealed and ultimately led to the U.S. Supreme Court ruling that segregation on public buses was unconstitutional. He became a prominent civil rights leader and harnessed the power of nonviolent mass protest to successfully challenge racial segregation.

On April 16, 1963, during one of his incarcerations, King wrote an open letter titled "Letter from Birmingham Jail," now considered a spiritual classic of world literature. He wrote the first part of the letter on the margins of a newspaper (the only paper available to him). Later more segments were penned on bits of paper provided by a jail trusty and a legal pad. His lawyers brought the fragments back to King's team who began compiling and editing it into the form we have today. In it he articulated that citizens have a moral responsibility to break unjust laws when they are oppressive to some groups of people, calling on them to take direct action rather than wait for a justice that may never materialize. This impulse ran deep in his Black Baptist heritage.

In the letter King called out his fellow clergyman for not bringing their bodies and voices to the struggle. "Injustice anywhere" he wrote, "is a threat to justice everywhere."[1] The letter is read and studied each year by

---

1. Martin Luther King Jr., "Letter from a Birmingham Jail," April 16, 1963, https://swap.stanford.edu/20141218230016/http://mlk-kpp01.stanford.edu/kingweb/popular_requests/frequentdocs/birmingham.pdf, 1.

millions of people. It is a foundational document for those engaged in the work of antiracism and social justice.

Each of King's arrests and imprisonments only further catalyzed and propelled the movement for racial equality.

In the famous speech we now call "I Have a Dream," King celebrated the glory of America's constitutional democracy, but compelled his audience to rethink America's commitment to its own ideals. King was able to cast a vision of the kingdom of God, and the possibility of peace and equality, while exposing the inconsistencies of the current discriminatory racial caste system. He gave voice to the struggles of an oppressed people, groaning beneath weight of racist laws and policies.

Throughout history, and particularly in the life of Dr. King, we can see the struggle to live the way of Jesus amid the randomness, disorder, and the chaos of systemic evil. King is an embodied witness of the kind of prophetic protest that is possible. While the work he began is by no means complete, his life and martyrdom made pathways for new possibilities.

King capably named the injustices faced by African American people, noting the church's complicity in those practices, while simultaneously lifting up a vision of hope for what could be. In a time of immense corruption and systemic evil, King led a movement that changed the world. The Civil Rights Movement offered safe harbor for millions of oppressed people. The movement worked against corruption and was structured to support people suffering blatant discrimination. The evil that King, and Baptists across history, prophetically confronted is not a new phenomenon.

When humanity rebelled against God, the mutability of creation was revealed, and sin, death, and evil entered the equation. A loving God immediately sought out beloved creation with the missional call, "Where are you?" (Gen 3:9). This is the cosmic narrative in which humanity has participated ever since. Furthermore, free will is not something unique to humanity; it characterizes all creatures and things, revealing an element of randomness. Rather than God micromanaging creation in a deterministic fashion, God is shaping a world with divine purposes and possibilities as humans emerge through the process of becoming.[2]

Sin is not simply rebellion against God but against creation. While epic goodness, beauty, and truth is baked into the "very good" creation, the universe as we currently know it is corrupted; not only does humanity need redemption, so does creation itself (Rom 8:22). Death, disease, and natural disasters (natural evil), as well as human evil flourishing in individuals, institutions, and systems (moral evil) are obvious features of our current sin-broken cosmos.

The historic position of Baptists in this scenario is non-violent prophetic protest and *withness*, which means faithful presence *with* the sufferer. Further, an unshakeable faith in a God of withness in a world of hurt.

Time for a Remix

"If God is good, how can there be so much suffering and evil in the world?" This is one of the most consistent and profound questions people wrestle with in our fresh expressions of church.

While I don't have a sufficient explanation for why there is suffering and evil in the world, Christians claim to experience God's sustaining presence in the midst of it. God somehow uses it, and more particularly as the church. . . we *are* sometimes God's answer to it. We partner with God to overcome the evil and suffering. Although I don't believe God causes suffering or evil to exist, they undeniably are pervasive forces throughout my life. As we learn to pioneer fresh expressions, we understand that there are questions and tragedies for which no answer will suffice, and yet we persist in the mystery.

I grew up in a world of strange dualisms: of light *and* dark, of mean streets *and* soft sanctuary pews, of ruthless victimizers *and* selfless saints,

---

2. Tyron Inbody, *The Faith of the Christian Church: An Introduction to Theology* (Grand Rapids, MI: Eerdmans, 2005), 155–57.

of deep hunger pains *and* extravagant potluck spreads. It was a very *good* world, but plagued with suffering and evil. I was born addicted, abandoned at birth, and my biological father unknown. My mother, a beautiful child of God, has fought a lifelong battle with addiction. When I was ten years old, my grandfather (that is, my adopted father) died of cancer. My grandmother, who introduced me to church, died in my arms several years later.

The local church of my childhood entered that dark journey and loved me within it. Even so, I squandered my early life with alcohol and dissolute living. I know well the path of suffering and evil. I walked it. I have felt the weight of institutional evil in an unjust economic machine that systematically oppresses some while a small minority profit from their suffering. I have felt the crushing desperation of poverty and abandonment. Ultimately, on the floor of a jailhouse while going through withdrawal, I cried out to Jesus in desperation. Christ came to me in a powerfully personal way that changed my life forever. I returned to the spiritual orphanage of my childhood, where a recovering alcoholic pastor nurtured me as a son.

More than sixteen years of continuous sobriety from all substances, years of therapy, spiritual direction, and mentorship has passed. I cannot forget those dark days, nor do I want to. Through that adversity God has forged me as a servant. Now I realize it's not my righteousness that God uses most powerfully; it's my brokenness. God does not cause suffering, but God has used mine to bring healing to others.

As an ordained pastor, I continuously encounter evil and the suffering that often results. I was present at the birth of a child, baptized her, then only weeks later conducted her memorial service when she died from blunt-force trauma. I have counseled victims of abuse, heard the confessions of abusers, and spent countless hours in the intensive-care units of hospitals and the final stop in hospice. I prayed for a young woman in her twenties as she died in the presence of her panic-stricken family. I watched cancer devastate faithful saints who loved God. I held the hand of a woman infected with AIDS in the final moments of her life as she called out for Jesus. I prayed over bewildered response teams deployed in the wake of devastating natural disasters, such as the hurricanes that ravage our state, or the earthquake in Haiti.

Honestly, in some of those situations I felt confused, inadequate, and speechless. I have also heard such well-meaning but misguided statements as, "Well, I guess God needed an angel" or "Nothing happens by mistake." Unwittingly, those who make such statements are contributing to an image of a tyrannical, micromanager God demanding blood and causing suffering.

So when bringing fresh expressions of ministry to those not currently connected to any church two aspects of God are held in creative tension: a temporal one, which is historical, relating, growing, and living, and one which is invulnerable, immutable.[3] God's triune power is demonstrated through a creating and transforming power, not through unilateral omnipotence. God's omnipotent power revealed in Jesus Christ is the power of withness and cruciform love, transforming death into rebirth, and making old creation "new creation."[4]

The Old Testament reveals the vulnerability and suffering of God, which are fully realized in the cross of Jesus. The cross breaks our old monarchial image of God and provides us with a new image, a crucified God who redeems us not by coercive power but by suffering *with us* in our suffering. David Hart warns against abstract answers in the midst of suffering.[5] Indeed, any level of "explanation" is not always comforting at the bedside of the sufferer.

In this world of darkness and light, I have seen the powerful way God's grace works among fallen realities. The church embodies "in its fallible, ambiguous way the transforming, healing power of Christ in the

3. Burton Cooper, *Why, God?* (Atlanta: John Knox, 1988), 80–90.

4. Inbody, *The Faith of the Christian Church,* 155–57.

5. David B. Hart, *The Doors of the Sea: Where Was God in the Tsunami?* (Grand Rapids, MI: Eerdmans, 2005), 99–100.

world."[6] The same church that plucked me from the darkness of my childhood is God's incarnate answer to suffering, a caring expression of Christ's redemptive power. We sing the love story of the cross.

Like Dr. King, our response is not one of simple explanation but of embodied *withness*. We point to a place where sin is overcome and peace is a real possibility, for Christ suffered the vilest form of evil, yet defeated death, and will return to fully do away with sin and suffering (Rev 21). We wait *with* the suffering, as the caring presence listening with hope, manifesting God's compassion and tears (liquid prayers) to extend the strength of divine presence.

We as the church can proclaim that "we have a dream" in which God's unconquerable love (Rom 8:31–39) and triune omnipotence will bring all things into renewal and perfection (Rev 21:5). This is one aspect of the historic legacy of the Baptist Church. Fresh Expressions is providing us a way to be the hands and feet of Jesus in a hurting world. Not by simply waiting back in our pristine buildings, but by joining our "other" in their suffering, where they live. We can link with God as we offer loving withness in a world of hurt. A love that has the potential to bring a little healing to the world.

Field Story

Sherry Krieger
Deacon, Assistant to the Bishop
for Strengthening Parishes and Synod Development
North West Ohio Synod-ELCA

The way of God does not require us to build churches and cathedrals, to make pilgrimages, to hear mass, and so on. God requires a heart moved by his grace. —*Martin Luther*

---

6. Cooper, *Why, God?* 15.

Fresh Expressions from the Lutheran perspective urges us to engage the world and encircle our neighbors with grace, love, and compassion.

Every one of us bears witness to a world that is deeply hurting; we see it daily. Taking seriously how Jesus engaged hurting people, we are called to follow his example. With a heart moved by God's grace, we are called to regularly, daily, individually, and corporately bring the grace, compassion, love, freedom, and justice of Jesus to hurting people and communities as we encounter them.

We have several developing Fresh Expressions in the Northwestern Ohio Synod of the Evangelical Lutheran Church in America (NWOS). *Fresh Bread* in Port Clinton, Ohio, started out in 2021 as an ecumenical endeavor by two pastors and a lay person to provide a different faith experience for people in the community. "Simple prayer, gentle music, and faith-based conversation over a free dinner" at a local Bistro has led to a regular and growing group that gathers monthly to share a meal and connect over faith conversations, whether their faith is strong, wavering, or nonexistent. Everyone is welcome and the meal is free. *Fresh Bread* is now responding to another pain point in the community and will be extending this Fresh Expression into the local children's services agency providing a meal, grace, hope, and faith with grandparents who are parenting their grandchildren.

In 2022, Mary lost her husband to a terminal illness. Living in a small town in northwest Ohio, she was faithful to her God, her church, and her husband through many long and lonely years of illness; she yearned for connections and community. Months later, now a widow, she shared her thoughts with some church women and friends in the community. Together they found their common pain: loneliness. They were caregivers or widows yearning for companionship. These women got together for an evening of fun and enjoyed it so much, they met together the next month, and the next month, and *Connections* was born. These women listened to each other, allowed the Holy Spirit to speak to them, and answered the inspiration to address the reality of loneliness in their community.

Connections is a Fresh Expression that connects caregivers and the community by encircling this holy group in the grace of Christ's love, companionship, fun, friendship, and a Jesus story that holds them together in faith. Anyone in the community is welcome. They may be hurting, lonely, or simply need engagement with others; there is a place for anyone at the table for *Connections'* annual community-wide picnic or their regular monthly gatherings.

With a heart moved by grace, NWOS leaders have listened and experienced the pain of their neighbors and have responded by experimenting with new spaces and forms of engagement that meet the needs, interests and pains of their community.

Missional Field Kit:
Searching for Sore Spots

What is sore in this community?

Following Paul's approach in Athens, conduct a "prayer walk" in your community with your team.[7] Perhaps use the people-map you created earlier. Plan a day for people to gather at your designated headquarters. Organize people in teams. Have others in the congregation cover you in prayer. Look for the "sore spots" in your community. Where do you see "hurt?" Ask yourselves, "God, what is breaking your heart in this community?" Do you have the boldness to pray, "Break our hearts for the things that break your heart"?

The key is to keep it simple. Focus on three basic practices: pray, observe, and encounter.

> **Prayer:** Have a conversation with God as you walk around together. Sensitize yourselves to the stirrings of the Holy Spirit: pray for specific homes, businesses, or schools. Pray over the streets, pray over the buildings, pray over the people.

---

7.   For in-depth guidance about prayer walks, see Sue Nilson Kibbey, *Ultimate Reliance: Breakthrough Prayer Practices for Leaders* (Nashville: Abingdon Press, 2019).

Observation: Pay attention to the context. This is simply a form of listening. How many people do you notice in the space? What are they doing? What are the conditions of the neighborhoods where you are? What kinds of isolation do you see? What kinds of practices are people participating in? Are people engaging each other in certain ways? How are they dressed? What ways do you see the Holy Spirit at work? What is God up to here?

Encounter: This is not about a Romans road, sinner's prayer, or any of that other business. Nor is it about holding up "Jesus Saves" signs or blowing on bull horns. When God brings someone into your path, and the Spirit nudges toward encounter, start with, "Hello. What's your name? How are you doing today?"

Have your team gather together to share observations. Have someone in the group write down the details. Perhaps use a white board so you can visualize it together. Agree to pray over these observations together until you meet again. You may rediscover that sore spots are the perfect places to cultivate fresh expressions of church.

Bible: Laying the Foundation

"The merciful Father will keep me in his Word so that I shall write or speak nothing but that which I can prove by Moses, the Prophets, the evangelists and other apostolic Scriptures and doctrines, explained in the true sense, Spirit and intent of Christ."[1]
—*Menno Simons*

A Catholic priest who had never read the Bible. That is not a jaded critique meant to offend, it is a statement of fact about Menno Simons. Simons consolidated and institutionalized the work initiated by previous moderate Anabaptist leaders and is considered the founder of the Mennonite Church. He also stood in a line of early reformers, like John Wycliffe, Jan Hus, Girolamo Savonarola, then Luther, Calvin, and Zwingli, who seemingly discovered the Bible again for the first time.

Simons was ordained a Dutch priest of the Catholic Church in Utrecht, Netherlands in 1524. 28 years old at his ordination, and although familiar with Greek and Latin and studied in Catholic doctrine, Simons had never read the Scriptures themselves. Simons later wrote, "I had not touched them during my life, for I feared if I should read them they would mislead me."[2]

---

1. Menno Simons, *The Complete Writings of Menno Simons*, trans, by L Verduin (Scottdale, 1956) 668 ff., 310, 159. Italics are the author's.

2. Simons, Menno. *My Confession*, 3. https://www.bernechristianfellowship.org/resources/Graphics/Tracts/My%20Confession%20-%20Menno%20Simons.pdf

In 1526, he began to seriously question the truthfulness of the Catholic doctrine of transubstantiation (a belief that the bread and wine transform into the actual flesh and blood of Jesus in the Eucharist). Simons "reluctantly" began to study the Bible. He concluded there was no Biblical warrant for the doctrine of transubstantiation. Yet, in the course of his study he believed he discovered the core protestant tenant of justification by grace through faith in Christ.

His open preaching about this quickly made him a controversial but popular speaker. Meanwhile, Huldrych Zwingli (1484–1531) was a leader of the Reformation in Switzerland. In 1519, Zwingli became the people's priest of the Grossmünster in Zürich. He began to preach ideas on reform of the Catholic Church. In his publications, he openly critiqued corruption in the ecclesiastical hierarchy, promoted clerical marriage, and attacked the use of icons in worship. He also took up expository preaching, going verse by verse through the Bible, a radical departure from Catholic mass.

Some of the followers of Zwingli's Reformed church thought that requiring church membership beginning at birth was inconsistent with the New Testament example, and that individuals should join only when willing to publicly acknowledge belief in Jesus and the desire to live in accordance with his teachings. At a small meeting in Zurich on 21 January 1525, Conrad Grebel, Felix Manz, and George Blaurock, along with twelve others, baptized each other. These baptisms marked the beginning of the Anabaptist movement. "Re-Baptizers" or "Anabaptists" using the Greek ana ["again"] were those who were rejecting infant baptism to receive a "believers' baptism."

This led to intense persecution of their movement throughout the sixteenth century. By 1530, most of the founding leaders had been killed for refusing to renounce their beliefs. *Martyrs Mirror* (1660), documents over 4,000 burnings of individuals, and numerous stonings, imprisonments, and live burials. Many were committed to pacifism, believing that God did not condone killing or the use of force for any reason, and the way of

Jesus was to forgive one's enemies. Their unwillingness to fight for their lives only compelled more people to consider their way.

After being rebaptized himself, Simons traveled extensively preaching the gospel, by explaining the Scriptures in an expository manner. Catholic officials were none too pleased with his activities. Emperor Charles V issued an edict against Simons, offering a significant bounty to anyone who might deliver him into the hands of authorities. Simons continued to exhort his fellow Anabaptist Reformers to reject violent means for accomplishing reform, advocating pacifism and separation from worldly power. The Mennonite World Conference was founded in Basel, Switzerland, in 1925 to celebrate the 400th anniversary of Anabaptism. In 2022, the organization had 109 member denominations in 59 countries, and 1.47 million baptized members in 10,300 churches. Today there are 2.1 million Anabaptists in the world, with multiple offshoots, many of whom consider Menno a spiritual forebearer.

Daily engagement with the Old and New Testaments is essential to the anabaptist tradition. Scriptural engagement and spiritual reading is the source of ongoing spiritual development. Mennonite Church USA states that from the beginning of the Anabaptist reformation in sixteenth-century Europe, Mennonites have sought to be a biblical people in ways that both borrowed from the Protestant reformation but is also distinct. Article 4 – Scripture, in the *Confession of Faith in a Mennonite Perspective*, states:

> We believe that all Scripture is inspired by God through the Holy Spirit for instruction in salvation and training in righteousness. We accept the Scriptures as the Word of God and as the fully reliable and trustworthy standard for Christian faith and life. We seek to understand and interpret Scripture in harmony with Jesus Christ as we are led by the Holy Spirit in the church.

> We believe that God was at work through the centuries in the process by which the books of the Old and New Testaments were inspired and written. Through the Holy Spirit, God moved human witnesses to write

what is needed for salvation, for guidance in faith and life, and for devotion to God.[3]

In this understanding of Scripture is a deep commitment to the Bible as the written word of God, but there is also the overarching understanding of Jesus as the Living Word, "Because Jesus Christ is the Word become flesh, Scripture as a whole has its center and fulfillment in him." This conviction flows back to Simons understanding of Hebrews 1:1-2, "In the past God spoke to our ancestors through the prophets at many times and in various ways, but in these last days he has spoken to us by his Son, whom he appointed heir of all things, and through whom also he made the universe."

That God had now spoken decisively in Jesus Christ led Menno to place the New Testament above the Old. Because God's purpose was fulfilled in the eternal Son, Menno said that Christ must be made central in every undertaking. Thus, all writing and preaching must be nothing other than Jesus Christ.

Most anabaptists hold to the Protestant Reformation doctrine of *sola scriptura*, meaning that claims on our understanding of Christian faith and life, such as tradition, culture, experience, reason, and political powers, need to be tested and corrected by the light of Holy Scripture.

Mennonites share the traditional Protestant emphasis on the authority of Scripture for doctrine and have underscored the following emphases:

- the authority of Scripture for ethics, for the relation of the church to society, and for church polity.

- the interpretation of Scripture in harmony with Jesus Christ, in the sense that his life, teachings, death, and resurrection are essential to understanding the Bible as a whole.

- the congregation of believers as the place where individual understandings and interpretations of Scripture are to be tested.

---

3. Article 4 – Scripture, in the Confession of Faith In a Mennonite Perspective

The Bible reveals God, enables us to develop faith, leads us to salvation (Rom 10:17), and calls us to be transformed into the character of God.

Followers in the Wesleyan way and speaking specifically of my denomination (The United Methodist Church) do not wave a *sola Scriptura* banner. "Wesley believed that the living core of the Christian faith was revealed in Scripture, illumined by tradition, vivified in personal experience, and confirmed by reason."[4] While it did not originate with Wesley, this interdependent fourfold matrix, now identified as the "quadrilateral," is a powerful tool for Methodists to employ in our theological task to "reflect upon God's gracious action in our lives."[5] In actuality, Mennonites and Methodists are closely aligned in our understanding of Scripture.

Regarding tradition, the United Methodist *Book of Discipline* states, "Christianity does not leap from New Testament times to the present as though nothing were to be learned from that great cloud of witnesses in between."[6] Christians always have been grappling with how to live out the gospel in a wide array of contexts. We draw from that depth of tradition by reaching back to the primitive church, including early creeds such as the Apostles' and Nicene-Constantinopolitan, various church councils, journeys of Christian pilgrims, and writings of Christian thinkers. This diverse witness has been preserved over the centuries. It contains the great triumphs and epic failures of our tradition, both from which we can learn.[7]

Our Christian experience also serves as a resource. Christian experience is "the personal appropriation of God's forgiving and empowering grace."[8] This highlights the necessary intersection of the Bible and our experience because "Our experience interacts with Scripture. We read Scripture in light of the conditions and events that help shape who we are,

4.   *The Book of Discipline, 2012* ¶104, p. 77.

5.   189. *The Book of Discipline, 2012* ¶104, p. 74.

6.   *The Book of Discipline, 2012,* ¶105, p. 83.

7.   Jones, *United Methodist Doctrine,*138–39.

8.   *The Book of Discipline, 2012* ¶105, p. 81.

and we interpret our experience in terms of Scripture."[9] Thus, while we read scripture through the lens of our own formation, the Bible interprets our life.

God also gave us wonderful brains. Our ability to reason is a gift from God (Luke 14:28). By reason, we hear and interpret the scripture, wrestle with its truth, and thoughtfully apply it to our lives. Reason, unfortunately, is marred by sin, and is best used in community with others.

One precious gift that Anabaptists and Methodists have left us is a particular interpretive tool for the study of scripture, that is—reading the whole of the Bible through the life, death, and resurrection of Jesus Christ. This tool has been called the "analogy of faith," or "analogy of Christ" or a "Jesus hermeneutic" (a method of interpretation). Paul Chilcote wrote, "This simply means that the Christian should read Scripture through the eyes of Christ or through the interpretive lens of the way of salvation. Jesus and the way of salvation through him become the measure of all things in terms of the meaning of the Bible."[10]

While each tradition may vary about the nature and interpretation of Scripture, we are unified in our agreement that it is the foundation for Christian life and thinking.

Time for a Remix

In a post-Christendom age, coping with toxic Christian ideologies such as nationalism, fundamentalism, and dispensationalism,[11] many people become "nones and dones," indeed even atheists, through reading the Bible. One of the primary roles of a cultivator of fresh expressions is to encounter people beyond the reach of the institutional church. The challenge is faithfully to interpret and recode the Bible in a way that people

---

9. *The Book of Discipline, 2012* ¶105, p. 85.

10. Paul W. Chilcote, *John and Charles Wesley: Selections from Their Writings and Hymns* (Woodstock, VT: SkyLight Paths Publications, 2011), 202.

11. See Paul W. Chilcote, *Active Faith: Resisting Four Dangerous Ideologies with the Wesleyan Way* (Nashville: Abingdon Press, 2019).

can understand and so that they can reorient their lives around its guidance for faith and practice.

Preaching and teaching the Bible in fresh expressions is a particularly exciting challenge. I appreciate the words of Walter Brueggemann, United Church of Christ theologian, and Old Testament scholar, who speaks of the prophet-poet's "shattering, evocative speech that breaks fixed conclusions and presses us always toward new, dangerous, imaginative possibilities. . . this artistic speech voiced in the prophetic construal of the Bible is the primary thrust of the church and its preaching."[12]

The Bible, when taught authentically, presents a counter-truth that challenges our reality. Furthermore, the process of discipleship, which comes from deep engagement with the Bible, involves learning to bend our lives to the instruction from scripture. Presbyterian minister, scholar, and author, Eugene Peterson wrote, "Christian spirituality is, in its entirety, rooted in and shaped by the scriptural text. . . . We are formed by the Holy Spirit in accordance with the text of Holy Scripture."[13]

However, in fresh expressions of church, scriptural engagement takes on many non-traditional contextually appropriate forms. Primarily, "sermons" are less about a single conductor leading an orchestra from the platform and more like the shared experience of an improvised jazz band. Rather than the "professional minister" teaching us what the Bible means, the sermon takes a communal form. We read a couple of verses, reflect upon what we've read, ask questions, and have a conversation. The community creates a sermonic experience together. Everyone has an opportunity to contribute. The people shape where the "sermon" goes.

Fresh expressions are not the place for written manuscripts, and in many cases not even a structured teaching plan. Studying the text in advance, knowing it deeply, being prepared to go where the people lead, are the skills required of pioneers. We have moved from monologues to

12. Walter Brueggemann, *Finally Comes the Poet* (Minneapolis: Fortress, 1989), 6–8.

13. Eugene Peterson, *Eat This Book: A Conversation in the Art of Spiritual Reading* (Grand Rapids, MI: Eerdmans, 2006), 15.

dialogues. We might be surprised to discover that scripted and monological sermons were not the norm across wider church history and cultures. They became the standard of proclamation primarily with the renaissance and the reformation.

Many scholars agree that the first apostles likely carried an oral tradition about Jesus for a period of time before the gospels came into written form. This treasury of stories about Jesus' life and teaching came to be known as the *kerygma*, related to the Greek verb κηρύσσω (kērússō), literally meaning "to cry or proclaim as a herald." The apostles traveled the ancient world proclaiming these stories about Jesus and inviting hearers to respond. This ultimately became the core of the early church's teaching about Jesus.

Further, the art of the sermonic conversation is not a new phenomenon. It is old—very old! This was in fact the preferred method of Jesus' own proclamation. Indeed, the idea of standing up delivering a carefully scripted monologue is foreign to the preaching of Jesus. The primary way that Jesus engaged the attention of his hearers was through telling stories, creating dialogues, and asking questions. Biblical scholar Martin Copenhaver reports that Jesus asked a total of 307 questions.

Jesus's parables are also a story-based form of questioning. They invite hearers to locate themselves in the parables. These stories are an intimate matter in the soul of the hearers, inviting even deeper questions, then and now.

When we examine Jesus's teaching form in this way, we can see where the dominant approach to preaching in the western church misses the mark. Most sermons spring from an interaction between the text and the preacher, with little-to-no input from the congregation.

Of course, when we open the sermonic forum to questions, the exploration will take unexpected twists and turns. This is indeed a different kind of skillset from those often associated with pulpit work in the inherited church. Even the most creative preachers are more skilled at presenting points than guiding a conversation. In some ways, scripted preaching

is the easy way out, rather than having to work through the actual reflections people have on the Bible.

In our various Fresh Expressions, we have taken a page from the early church's playbook regarding the *kerygma*. Perhaps their strategy for a pre-Christian world can be adapted to a post-Christian world?

We train our laity to do a simple version of the apostolic practice in home, work, and third places where these small contextual Christian communities gather. Many people who participate can't or don't want to attend more traditional forms of church, so we incarnate church with them where they are. These gatherings promote open and honest conversations about the joys and struggles in our lives.

In the context of these conversations, we share "Jesus Stories," simple, short, retellings about something Jesus said or did in five minutes or less. We equip our laity with simple questions to frame the conversations: What would this story look like today? What if this Jesus story is true? If it is true, how would it make a difference in my life? What is this Jesus story saying to me? What is one small thing I can change in my daily life because of this Jesus story? What is one thing I might do differently? These questions give access for non-Christians to join in the conversation. They are intentionally designed not to be questions with "right" or "wrong" answers, but to invite curiosity and reflection.

Burritos and Bibles, mentioned earlier, is the fresh expression that meets at Tijuana Flats, where we study the scripture inductively and conclude with Holy Communion. This gathering aggregates folks from a variety of perspectives across the theological spectrum. We began with four people and now fill the restaurant. For some who are not ready to participate in traditional "church" but willing to have a burrito, all-you-can-eat chips and salsa, and seek to better understand the Bible—this is their church. I love exploring together and watching how the Spirit often enlightens us through communal study.

Some of our fresh-expression leaders lean more Calvinist in theology than Wesleyan. Some have no theological orientation at all. We try to encourage theological unity but not theological uniformity. We love the same Lord and often share our different perspectives. This brings us all to fuller understanding (Prov 27:17). However, while we may mostly agree that the biblical authors wrote under the inspiration of the Holy Spirit (2 Tim 3:16-17), we have some distinctions on exactly how the Bible is God's Word or contains God's word, that is, how the Bible is true.

I believe God inspired the authors of the scriptures, and that God worked through the process of editing, compiling, and canonization (which means establishing the books that are authorized for faith and practice). God continues to work in us now as we read. When I prepare, first I pray for the Spirit to illuminate my understanding of the text. However, I struggle with a literal interpretation of the Bible as "infallible and inerrant." I find these to be claims the Bible doesn't actually make for itself.

Here I appropriate the "analogy of faith" or the "Jesus hermeneutic" mentioned above. Jesus understood Scripture as *authoritative*. He quoted Hebrew Bible texts often and claimed that his mission was to "fulfill" them (Matt 5:17). Yet his fulfillment, in some cases, is quite radical. This is made clear by his confrontations with the Pharisees (compare Deut 24:1 with Mark 10:2-9) and the "fulfillment" teachings: "you've heard it said. . . but I say." Jesus expands "eye for an eye" *to* "turn the other cheek," and "hate your enemies" *to* "love your enemies and pray for them" (Matt 5:17-48).

Further, Jesus himself directly reframes sections in the Book of Leviticus that speak of "clean versus unclean" sins that require the death penalty, and the seemingly crude restrictions concerning those with birth defects, or the commandment that menstruating women are not allowed in community worship. Also, even among the various accounts of the resurrection, the most profound moment in history, there are inconsistencies. Hence, I see Jesus as "the lens and filter of the *definitive* and *unmitigated* word of God" through which all of the Old and New Testaments should be read and understood.[14]

Thus, the authority of scripture is not based simply around a grouping of rules we must follow. This authority legitimates our mission. Authority authorizes our freedom to act within boundaries. From Genesis to Revelation, that mission starts with "Where are you?" and finds fulfillment in Christ—God eternally *with us*. The whole Bible points to Jesus Christ.

In confessing the scriptures together as the church, we become that Christ-centered community of which it speaks. The message it contains is true, as is the God it reveals. Hence, the Bible is true in a way that nothing else can be, because it introduces us to the one who is "the way, the *truth*, and the life" (John 14:6) (emphasis mine). The centerpiece of fresh expressions ministry is its innovative proclamation in contextually accessible ways.

Field Story
Rev. Gordon Cook
Giving God Time and Clothing Bank Congregation
The Drive Baptist Church
Fredericton, New Brunswick, Canada

What began as a response to a request from a local elementary school for winter coats, hats, and mittens for their less fortunate students has now resulted in a Fresh Expressions Community called "Giving God Time," located in Fredericton, New Brunswick, Canada. In Eastern Canada, the winter months are cold, snowy, and often harsh. Due to sub-zero Celsius temperatures and the socioeconomic demographics of our community, the local elementary school reached out to us, The Drive Baptist Church, to see if we would collect winter clothes for children who were in desperate

---

14. Adam Hamilton, *Making Sense of the Bible: Rediscovering the Power of Scripture Today* (New York: HarperOne, 2014), 164–66; 175.

need. This request, dating back to 2001, inspired a few faithful church members to start collecting clothing in the basement of our church.

Over time, a few tables of winter clothes grew into a free clothing and food distribution program that services clients of all ages from across the city. Dozens of volunteers prepare and give away literal tons of clothing and food every year. What came as a revelation to us was that through the meeting of these needs, God was creating a new community. Relationships were forming, trust was being built, and time was being shared. We even began serving breakfast as people were "shopping": the community was beginning to blossom.

In 2019, a member of our denomination's staff (CBAC) paid a visit to the Clothing Bank. Upon witnessing all that was going on, he declared, "Can you see it! Look! There is a congregation here. I see Church happening!" As we observed this together, he asked me if I had ever heard of Fresh Expressions. He explained to me how new forms of congregations were meeting in city parks, restaurants, bars, gyms, and even tattoo parlors. That is when we began wondering if God could form a new Christ-centered congregation at a Clothing Bank in Fredericton.

A few months later, "Giving God Time" was born. The name was chosen because it was very obvious to us that we serve a "Giving God." We also felt we needed to provide this new community with an opportunity to give of themselves to God, thus, "Giving God Time." We were convicted that this time should be accessible to everyone, regardless of faith experience. Instead of using terms like praise, prayer, or Bible study, we were led to have this group give God their Appreciation (Praise), Anxieties (Prayer), and Attention (Bible Study). That is the outline for every "Giving God Time" service, which is held weekly for twenty minutes, prior to the opening of the clothing bank. We began with 3-5 people meeting together, growing to an average of 12. When Covid-19 intervened for a lengthy season, the community seemed to scatter. Once we were able to reconvene, we returned to 3-5 attenders. Since then, the Lord has blessed this congregation with an average of 25 attenders over the past year. This has become a gateway for many people, from various backgrounds and cultures, to discover and return to an active faith in Christ and fellowship within a community of believers. What began as a simple request to help a local school in need has now become a vibrant community of faith—one driven to see God's Kingdom unfold in fresh and tangible ways.

Missional Field Kit: Engaging Scripture with "Nones and Dones"

How do we study the Bible with people who have little to no experience with it?

Michael Moynagh and I suggest a set of simple questions to introduce someone to Jesus through Bible study. You could choose one Jesus story, read it together, and each week simply ask one of the following questions:

1. If this story happened today, what would it look like?

2. What does this story say to you?

3. How could this story make a difference in my life?

4. How did it make a difference?

Grace-Filled Waters and Open Table

Contrary to popular belief, the first Methodist Fresh Expression was not started by John or Charles Wesley, but rather their mother Susanna . . . in her kitchen.

Many call her the "Mother of Methodism," but her influence has been historically downplayed. Yes, she raised ten children, including John, Charles, and Mehetabel (a notable poet in her own right), but there's more to the story.

In 1710 Susanna began conducting irregular worship services in her home. A nine-year-old John Wesley grew up in this environment of ecclesial innovation. Susanna, deeply committed to the inherited church, also saw its ineffectiveness. She broke many social and ecclesiastical conventions of her time.

Here are a couple of exerpts from some of her personal letters to her husband, Samuel Wesley, himself a priest who travelled frequently, spent time in debtors' prison, and struggled to provide financially for the family. He asked her to stop these irregular gatherings as they were upsetting the local curate Rev Inman (who by all accounts was less than effective).

February 6, 1712

"I am a woman, so I am also mistress of a large family. And though the superior charge of the souls contained in it lies upon you as head of the family and as their minister, yet in your absence I cannot but look upon every soul you leave under my care as a talent committed to me under a trust by the great Lord of all the families of heaven and earth. And if I am unfaithful to him or to you in neglecting to improve these talents, how shall I answer unto him, when he shall command me to render an account of my stewardship?"

Describing how the gatherings started with a kind of personal family chapel for the kids, then evolved from there...

"This was the beginning of my present practice: other people coming in and joining with us was purely accidental. Our lad told his parents— they first desired to be admitted; then others who heard of it begged leave also; so our company increased to about thirty and seldom exceeded forty last winter."

Sound like the fresh expression journey? This was alongside an inherited congregation that worshiped at about 20 people...

"With those few neighbours who then came to me I discoursed more freely and affectionately than before. I chose the best and most awakening sermons we had, and I spent more time with them in such exercises. Since this our company has increased every night, for I dare deny none that asks admittance. Last Sunday I believe we had above two hundred, and yet many went away for want of room..."

Yes. Susanna Wesley planted a church in her home in which 200+ people were gathering!

Some excerpts from her follow up letter to Samuel, February 25, 1712:

"but 'tis plain in fact that this one thing has brought more people to church than ever anything did in so short a time."

Not only were new people connecting in her house church, but they were beginning to be involved in the life of the inherited church as well.

"If you do after all think fit to dissolve this assembly, do not tell me any more that you desire me to do it, for that will not satisfy my conscience; but send me your positive command in such full and express terms as may absolve me from all guilt and punishment for neglecting this opportunity of doing good to souls, when you and I shall appear before the great and awful tribunal of our Lord Jesus Christ. I dare not wish this practice of ours had never been begun, but it will be with extreme grief that I shall dismiss them, because I foresee the consequences. I pray God direct and bless you."

Translation: if you want to stop this, do it yourself, but these souls will be on your hands!

Susanna had turned her kitchen into an *open table* for the community. I can't help but wonder how growing up in this environment of ecclesial innovation would have impacted the young Wesley boys. Watching their mother start a new faith community in the kitchen, an irregular practice, frowned upon by the church and their own father.

This is part of the treasured inheritance of the people called Methodists. A people wired for the blended ecology, in which new innovative forms of church spring up alongside existing congregations.

The Methodist story begins at an open table.

John Wesley considered the sacraments to be filled with mystery and the "ordinary channels through which God might convey to us. . . grace."[1] Methodists agree with many Protestants across the theological spectrum that "There are two sacraments ordained of Christ our Lord in the Gospel; that is to say Baptism and the Supper of the Lord."[2] Catholic siblings uphold seven sacraments in the Church: Baptism, Confirmation or Chrismation, Eucharist, Penance, Anointing of the Sick, Holy Orders, and Matrimony.

Wesley was convinced that the scriptural ordination of the two sacraments originated with Christ himself. Jesus commands his disciples to

---

1. John Wesley, *The Standard Sermons in Modern English*, ed. K. C. Kinghorn, (Nashville: 2002), vol. 1, 264.

2. *The Book of Discipline, 2012* ¶103: XVI.

"go therefore and make disciples" by "baptizing them in the name of the Father and of the Son and of the Holy Spirit" (Matt 28:19 NRSV). Jesus instructs the disciples to partake of this meal (Matt 26:17; Mark 14:12; Luke 22:17) "in remembrance of me" (Luke 22:19; 1 Cor 11:24). Since the very first apostles, entrance through baptism was immediately followed with devotion "to the apostles' teaching, to the community, to their shared meals, and to their prayers" (Acts 2:41-42). Table fellowship has always been the center of Christian community and continues to be in fresh expressions of church.

The sacraments, as "outward signs of inward grace," are tangible objects highlighting spiritual realities. The grace-filled waters of our baptism wash us clean, herald our new birth as children of God, and empower us to transform the world. True life begins in the waters of our baptism. The grace-saturated meal presents our continual need for God and nourishes us for the journey. Bread and grape juice symbolize the graceful God who took on flesh and blood and "moved into the neighborhood" (John 1:14 MSG). I often explain the sacraments as ordinary presents, with extraordinary presence. These ordinary elements, infused with the Holy Spirit, point to the extraordinary nature of God's grace and mysterious activity in our lives. God engages our senses in each sacrament. In baptism, we see and hear the water trickling, and we feel it wash over us. In Holy Communion, we touch and taste the bread and juice as we search our hearts and confess our brokenness.

Besides the grace-filled dimension of baptism that precedes our own awareness, one distinct Wesleyan emphasis is the *open table*.

For Wesley, Holy Communion was in one sense a sacrament of maintenance in which we *remember* our unification with Christ. Like many other Protestants, Methodists see communion as more than a remembrance and short of transubstantiation, the Spirit makes the presence of Christ real in the elements. We partake, we drink, and we eat of his own living presence which sanctifies and sustains us (John 6:56-58). In a mysterious way, our spirits are nourished as grace is conveyed to us. We begin with confession and pardon, as we acknowledge "we have rebelled against your love."[3] And because Wesley believed this can be a moment of conversion, Holy Communion is a missional phenomenon.[4] Early Christians gathered around this meal in public spaces (1 Cor 11:17-34). Paul reminds us when we partake, it is a καταγγέλλω or *proclamation*: "you proclaim the Lord's death until he comes" (1 Cor 11:26 NRSV).

It is a frequent occurrence in fresh expressions that people receive Christ through partaking in the Lord's Supper for the first time. We've heard something to the effect of, "When I tore the bread, I realized Christ died for me," many times. The graceful meal can both spark faith and sustain it. Further, an open table means that all are welcome no matter what their status may be.[5] Our inclusivity is based on the radical table fellowship of Jesus himself (Matt 9:10; Luke 15:2). No one is "worthy" to receive.[6] "We confess that we have not loved you with our whole heart. . . . We have not heard the cry of the needy."[7] It is a feast of forgiveness and acceptance, a foretaste of God's kingdom open to all sinners where we proclaim three essential truths: "Christ has died; Christ is risen; Christ will come again."[8] It is one of the channels through which this relentless, seeking God initiates a relationship with us.

These Wesleyan distinctives provide incredible missional potential for Fresh Expressions of Church, as well as some unique challenges. In Wesley's own day, there was serious controversy around lay preachers attempting to administer sacraments, something they had no authority to do under Anglican ecclesial authority.

---

3. *The United Methodist Hymnal*, p. 12.

4. Runyon, *The New Creation*, 134.

5. Charles Wesley proclaims in "Come, Sinners, to the Gospel Feast": "let every soul be Jesus' guest. Ye need not one be left behind, for God hath bid all humankind" (no. 339 in *The United Methodist Hymnal*, st. 1).

6. Charles Wesley, "Come Sinners, to the Gospel Feast": "the invitation is to all. Come, all the world! Come, sinner thou!" st. 2.

7. *United Methodist Hymnal*, 12.

8. *United Methodist Hymnal*, 14.

Time for a Remix

In Methodist circles, handling of the sacraments continues to be an area of contention. Often in our national trainings, people get to the *consecration dilemma*: "So if most people leading fresh expressions are laity, who is serving communion and conducting the baptisms?" The response to this question must be contextually sensitive.

Let's start with the Lord's Supper. Different traditions have different ideas about this, so I want to be careful not to make universal prescriptions. For instance, some are fine with an ordained person "pre-consecrating" the elements before they are taken to the location. Others want the ordained person to be present during the gathering. Some churches are quite creative, taking the left-over elements from the traditional worship experiences and allowing the cultivators to serve them in the fresh expressions. If possible, having an ordained person is ideal; however, for churches that have multiple fresh expressions this may be unrealistic.

Regarding baptism, it doesn't seem like much of a challenge to get an ordained individual to preside. In many churches, baptisms are rare occasions.

For instance, in my role as cultivator of fresh expressions for the Florida Conference, I have observed this reality firsthand. In 2017, the FLUMC was comprised of six hundred twenty-five+ churches (+ correlates with multi-site scenarios). Of these, four hundred seventy-two churches were flat or declining in Average Worship Attendance (AWA) over the previous five years. Two hundred forty-two churches lost twenty percent of their membership, and two hundred seventy-two reported one or no baptisms. Three hundred four of the churches who lost AWA are in areas where the population is growing. In 2018, five hundred ninety-three church entities reporting End of Year Statistics. Of those, 64 percent were flat or declined in membership, and 69 percent were flat or declined in average worship attendance.[9]

---

9. Email correspondence with Steve Loher, Florida UMC Manager of Knowledge and Information Services on April 9, 2019.

In 2024 these trends have continued and after an intense season of disaffiliation, 380 churches remain in The Florida Conference. This has caused a realignment of the districts from eight to six districts. The redrawing of district lines is in response to the reality of the loss of 35 percent of our churches in the last few years. Yet alongside this narrative of decline is a hopeful story of the over 300 Fresh Expressions of Church that have started even amid the challenges of the pandemic and disaffiliation.

Reaching and making new Christians is a pervasive challenge. These troubling statistics are not unique. Of the approximately thirty-three thousand United Methodist congregations in the US, only five, or .01 percent, have been able to maintain an annual growth rate of 10 percent for the past ten years.[10] When people aren't being baptized into the faith, churches will decline.

Yet, there are some more positive developments in Florida as well. While at this point extraneous variables make it impossible to directly correlate fresh expressions activity with the revitalization of inherited congregations, some congregations are growing in worship attendance. Close to half of those growing congregations in the North Central District (41 percent) have been experimenting with fresh expressions for the past four years. Each of those experimenting congregations grew in "professions of faith" and baptisms. They are among a handful of churches who are reversing decline by growing primarily through reaching out to the "nones" and forming new Christians.[11]

The struggle over sacraments may be a little bit of history rhyming. Regarding Methodism, some have argued that the issue of sacraments actually led to the creation of a new denomination rather than a renewal movement within the larger church. As mentioned, not only did lay preachers serve the sacraments, but Wesley also himself conducted ordinations outside the proper Anglican ecclesial channels.

---

10. Len Wilson, "Top 25 Fastest Growing Large United Methodist Churches, 2017 Edition," *lenwilson.us.* January 10, 2017, http://lenwilson.us/top-25-fastest-growing-large-umc-2017/.

11. Executive Summary. Collected for FLUMC NCD 2018 Imprint Report.

Perhaps it is time for people in the Wesleyan tradition to rethink the idea of itinerant clergy serving circuits? Rather than understanding itineration in the institutional sense of being sent annually from one local church to another, local clergy now find themselves in communities where these strange circuits of fresh expressions are emerging. The ordained clergy could share the joy of visiting these emerging churches to provide the sacramental authority necessary. This is already starting to happen in high fresh expressions areas.

I'm convinced that when we have an institutional log jam in sharing these grace-filled sacraments with all people, there are harder questions to ask. While I can't make general prescriptions for the whole church, I can share how we are navigating these challenges in the church I now lead, which is a traditional congregation and a network of fresh expressions.

Field Story
Yurt Missional Community
Revd. Sue Hughes
Anglican Pioneer Curate, St Mary's Risborough, UK
Mission Supporter for the Oxford Diocese

The Yurt Missional Community grew out of a traditional and rural market town parish, St Mary's & St Peter's in Princes Risborough, Buckinghamshire.

Early in the Covid-19 pandemic, my husband made a cross from an ash tree and put it outside our home beside the road. During the pandemic, when every church was closed, we offered a place for people to write prayers on tags and hang them on the tree and know that God would somehow see them, and that there would be someone praying on their behalf.

It has been so beautiful and humbling. Walkers, cyclists, or even people driving past stop and write something on a tag and hang it on the tree cross. These are their deepest heart cries to God, and we have the privilege of praying for them.

When the pandemic had passed, and following several unusual and fruitful conversations with walkers and people who had just turned up at church, we decided to offer an "Alpha" course in the yurt. It was a small group of thirteen to fifteen people, and we meet weekly for six weeks.

With the help of the Holy Spirit, we were able to listen, love, and build community in a short time, and this group of "pilgrims" were more than keen to continue meeting. One of the members lovingly named us "the Yurties," which has stuck with us and everyone at the "mother" church.

We have continued to meet weekly and have explored the spiritual disciplines to enable us to grow as disciples to Jesus. We are a neurodiverse group, and our worship always reflects us as a community. Each group member is encouraged and supported to lead the weekly worship and offer hospitality.

The invitation is to lead this special time together, from our own authentic place of worship with God. Worship may look like drawing pictures together; lying on the floor in silence; making with paper and glue, listening to music, singing, or listening to the rain fall on the canvas. We are blessed through the richness of our individuality in worship, as we are made in the image of a loving creator God.

We have developed a communal practice of prayer, formed out of a week of prayer and hospitality, which led to a permanent prayer rhythm, early morning before people head off to work. This has shaped and fueled who we are and birthed a new missional community.

We have "Yurt Sailors" who lead sessions and have pastoral oversight. Their job description: "If you want to build a ship, don't drum up people together to collect wood and don't assign them tasks and work, but rather teach them to long for the endless immensity of the sea."[12]

The Yurt Community has recently received PCC (parish church council) approval for the start of a new missional community called "Maker & Fixer," which has come from prayer, relationship-building, and discernment amongst a repair barn community and a Ukrainian community.

---

12. Antoine de Saint-Exupéry

The Maker & Fixer Community will "create belonging, confidence, and community collaboration at the Culverton Barns using sustainability and 'maker & fixer' skills to proclaim the Good News of the Kingdom," beginning in Spring 2024!

Our story is that we have a God who can repair, restore, and make all things new!

"Behold, I am doing a new thing; now it springs forth, do you not perceive it? I will make a way in the wilderness and rivers in the desert" (Isa 43:19).

Missional Field Kit:
Some Remixing

1. With your team, write out a list of common items in the church that have symbolic meaning. Perhaps do a field trip in the sanctuary. A list may include: Cross, Organ, Hymnal, Candles, Pew, Altar, Robes, Offering Envelope, Guitar, Drums, *Book of Common Worship*, *Book of Discipline*, Laptop, Speaker, Chalice, Umbrellas, and so on.

2. Pair up in teams and try to create as many alternative uses for these items as possible. Take two minutes for each item (For instance, hymnal: doorstop, weapon, height increaser, scrap paper, kindling, yard ornament, closet filler, and so on)

3. Discern together as a team: What other symbolic meaning might those items have for people outside the church?

4. Using only items familiar to those outside the church, what items might have symbolic meaning for them? (For instance, football, racecar, iPhone, coffee cup, instruction manual, lawn mower, movie theater seat, barstool, and so on). How might you build bridges of meaning between those symbols? Or how might you translate the meaning of the items of the church world to the items of their world?

A Mission with a Church, Not a Church with a Mission

In the sixteenth and seventeenth centuries the idea that national unity was linked with religious uniformity collapsed. The 1600's were a time when England was embroiled in civil war. The bloodshed can be traced back to political tensions between Royalists and Parliamentarians. From 1639 to 1653 the Wars of the Three Kingdoms, consisted of the First English Civil War, the Second English Civil War, and The Anglo-Scottish War of 1650 to 1652 (sometimes referred to as the *Third English Civil War*).

While the conflicts between the three kingdoms of England, Scotland and Ireland had similarities, each also had distinct issues and objectives. The First English Civil War was fought primarily over power struggle between Parliament and Charles I. That war ended in June 1646 with Royalist defeat and the king in custody. The Second English Civil War ultimately resulted in the execution of Charles I in January 1649, and the establishment of the Commonwealth of England. Around 100,000 people died in battle, tens of thousands more were captured, and around 127,000 non-combat deaths included some 40,000 civilians.

In 1650, Charles II was crowned king of Scotland, and he agreed to create a Presbyterian church in both England and Scotland. Presbyterianism is a Reformed Protestant tradition named for its form of church government by representative assemblies of elders. The word is derived from the Biblical Greek πρεσβύτερος (presbýteros), one who served as an elder. Presbyterianism refers primarily to the system of church government by representative assemblies called presbyteries, in contrast to government by bishops (episcopal system), or by congregations (congregationalism). Many Reformed churches are organized in a similar way, but the word Presbyterian is applied to churches that trace their roots to the Church of Scotland or to English Dissenter groups that formed during the Wars of the Three Kingdoms.

Presbyterian tradition, through the Church of Scotland, traces its early roots back to Saint Columba, through the sixth-century Hiberno-Scottish mission. They retained Celtic features and practiced a form of monasticism. The Church in Scotland maintained the Christian feast of Easter at a date different from the See of Rome until at the Synod of Whitby in 664, ruled that Easter would be celebrated according to the Roman date, not the Celtic date. Although Roman influence would eventually dominate the Church in Scotland, certain Celtic influences were preserved.

The Presbyterian Church was formed in the crucible of a society plagued with suffering, political upheaval, and war, much of which flowed back to the tensions between different expressions of church, and how those traditions related to the monarchy. Reformed Christians emerged from within a tension between obedience to civil authority and critical evaluation of it.

Presbyterians were among the first Reformed immigrants to arrive in America. They settled along the East Coast, and then pushed westward into the American wilderness. Presbyterian congregations were founded as early as the 1630s, and in 1706, seven Presbyterian ministers formed the first Presbyterian presbytery in the new colonies. Presbyterians played a role in developing the founding documents of the United States, particularly the Religion Clauses in the Constitution and the wording of the First Amendment. Freedom of religion is protected by the Establishment Clause and Free Exercise Clause, which together form the religious liberty clauses of the First Amendment.

Presbyteries consisted of the clergy and appointed lay representatives from a particular geographical area. The presbytery appoints ministers to vacant pulpits, enforces church discipline, and monitors the financial state of congregations. They also educate ministers and laity. Presbyterianism was a distinct stream within the larger Protestant Reformation, especially influenced by the French theologian John Calvin (1509–1564), known for the development of Reformed theology. John Knox (1514–1572), who studied with Calvin in Geneva, was a Scottish minister, Reformed theologian, and founder of the Presbyterian Church of Scotland.

One profound gift from the Presbyterian understanding of evangelism, missions, and church planting is the centrality of the church in this strategy. Modern evangelicalism has often construed these activities as an individualistic endeavor. Evangelists are those individuals who "win people to Christ" in one-on-one encounters or in mass within stadiums. Presbyterians have historically insisted upon the importance of the congregation itself in evangelistic efforts.

The Westminster Confession of Faith states the importance of the church in regards to mission, evangelism, and planting:

> The visible church, which is also catholic or universal under the gospel (not confined to one nation, as before under the law), consists of all those throughout the world that profess the true religion; and of their children: and is the kingdom of the Lord Jesus Christ, the house and family of God, out of which there is no ordinary possibility of salvation.[1]

God has a mission; thus, there is a church. The church does not have a mission; it is God's missional instrument.[2] "Mission does not come from

---

1. Westminster Confession of Faith, 25.2.

2. Stephen B. Bevans and Roger Schroeder, *Prophetic Dialogue: Reflections on Christian Mission Today* (Maryknoll, NY: Orbis, 2011), 15.

the church; it is from mission and in light of mission that the church has to be understood."[3] The church flows from the mission of God, "mission . . . is prior to the church, and is constitutive of its very existence."[4] Mission should birth structures, as mission takes shape so does the church. Structures should enable mission.

Early Presbyterianism was the "missional church" movement of its day. Thus, the structure and polity of the presbytery was born in the process of mission. Ultimately missionary need, and an evolving social context, gave rise to different forms of order.

The origins of the Episcopal Church also lie in the violent religious disagreements of sixteenth century Europe. The English church had initially split from Rome under the questionable motivations of King Henry VIII. Doctrinal division, wars, and civil unrest followed. The first Anglican service in North America occurred when Sir Francis Drake's crew landed just north of San Francisco Bay in 1579. Sir Walter Raleigh attempted to found a colony in what is now North Carolina in 1589. However, the first Anglican parishes were established with the Virginia Colony in the years following 1607.

Anglicanism progressed generally from South to North among the coastal American colonies. It was Charles II (1660–1685) who established Anglicanism in Maryland, and six counties of New York. More Anglican parishes began to appear in Pennsylvania, Massachusetts, Connecticut, and New Jersey by the end of the seventeenth century. Puritanism was established primarily in the northern colonies, Rhode Island was strongly Baptist, and Catholicism was strong in Maryland.

Following the American Revolution, Church of England congregations in the newly independent States reorganized themselves as a new church. This church would be free from both the monarchy and episcopal oversight by English bishops. The new church organized as "Episcopal"

---

3. Jürgen Moltmann, *The Church in the Power of the Spirit: A Contribution to Messianic Ecclesiology* (Minneapolis: Fortress, 1993), 10.

4. Stephen B. Bevans and Roger P. Schroeder, *Constants in Context* (Maryknoll, NY: Orbis, 2004), 13.

to maintain the historic polity of bishops, priests and deacons. However, it adapted its constitution from English Bishops appointed by a monarch to elected bishops. English bishops continue even now to be appointed by the monarch. Episcopalians also played a part as founders of America's new government. Some signed the Declaration of Independence and facilitated the services for the inauguration of George Washington.

These missional adaptations allowed for a contextual church to flourish in a new space and era. Today, among the Anglican Communion, members are known both as "Episcopalians" and "Anglicans." The Episcopal Church is one of 30 autonomous national churches that are part of the Anglican Communion. Now, with 70 million members in 64,000 congregations in 164 countries, the Anglican Communion is the third largest body of Christians in the world, following after the Roman Catholic and Eastern Orthodox communions.

Perhaps this is even an understatement of Anglicanism's reach. John Wesley did not see Methodism as a separate church, but a renewal movement within the Church of England, which he served faithfully as an ordained clergyperson until the day he died. Episcopal Bishop George Sumner writes, "In mission, we are all Methodists now, at least in our root assumptions and many of our strategies." He notes how Wesleyan missiological DNA is deeply embedded in global Anglicanism, as a set of common features: "Lay leadership, Going out to where people are, Evangelistic gatherings, Small groups, Confession, Converted hearts, Singing" have been remixed in many contextual variations.[5] Thus, a common heritage between Wesleyanism and Anglicanism have led to discussions for full communion among the Episcopal Church and The United Methodist Church.

Each of these movements reappropriated the first principles of scripture around leadership. While there is disagreement about one clear biblical blueprint regarding church order, there is agreement that missionary

---

5. Sumner, George. "Wesley and Anglican Mission." 2014. https:// livingchurch. org/2014/10/14/wesley-and-anglican-mission/

need precipitates new forms of church. Perhaps here we can lean into the tradition of the early church fathers. In the scriptural allusions we see the terms *bishop* and *elder* used to describe local church leaders interchangeably. Ignatius of Antioch, writing just before his martyrdom in 110 CE, shows us how the threefold leadership arrangement functioned in the early church. In his letters, we discover that each local church had the same structure, with a bishop, assisted by a group of presbyters or elders, together with a group of deacons.[6] These positions were localized within each congregation. So there is room for interpretation here, and each form of church structure can be argued from both Scripture and tradition. What unifies Christians across these differences is a common mission to make disciples of all the world, and to let that purpose guide the formation of our polity.

To truly become a "mission with a church" some rule *blend*ing seems necessary for inherited and emerging modes of church to live together.

Time for a Remix

Archbishop Rowan Williams used his role to foster the seeding of the Fresh Expressions movement in the UK. He coined the phrase a "mixed economy of church." Williams also frequently exclaims, "It's not the Church of God that has a mission, but the God of mission who has a church." The Fresh Expressions movement is awakening an instrumental understanding of the church again. It is not God's job to serve the church; the church is an instrument in the hand of a missionary God.

In the Fresh Expressions movement, we return to a minimalist definition of the church, based primarily in the "first principles" of scripture. These essential "marks" were formalized in the Nicene Creed in 381 CE as *one, holy, apostolic, catholic.* In fresh expressions language, we appropriate

---

6. Marcellino D'ambrosio, *When the Church Was Young: Voices of the Early Fathers* (Cincinnati, OH: Servant Books, 2014), 26.

and remix those words to speak of the essentials as *inward, upward, outward,* and *ofward.*

> **Inward:** a community of believers unified *in* the faith, living *in* the one Lordship of Jesus Christ.

> **Upward:** we grow *up* in worship of the God of unfailing love, seeking to reflect God's own character through our love for God and neighbor.

> **Outward:** a community sent *out* in mission to the world together.

> **Ofward:** we belong to a universal connection *of* Christians throughout all space, time, race, and nation.

Denominations have taken the three scriptural leadership roles of elder, bishop, and deacon, and arranged them in a pyramidal corporate hierarchy. Steven Croft advocates for a rediscovery of the value of these three leadership roles in a local context. He associates the three groups in the following way

1. Deacon (*diakonia*) the servant ministry of the church with pioneers;

2. Elder (*presbyteros*) or priestly function of the church enabling and sustaining both inherited and emerging forms of church;

3. Bishop (*episcope*) the watching-over function of the church, those who exercise collaborative oversight of areas with multiple parishes.

He also argues that we continue to need lay, licensed, and ordained individuals, for the full health of the mixed economy.[7] Local clergy persons overseeing inherited congregations and networks of fresh expressions need

---

7. Steven J. Croft, *The Future of the Parish System: Shaping the Church of England for the Twenty-first Century* (London, UK: Church House, 2006), 78–90.

to understand themselves again as quasi-bishops, whose role is to equip the whole people of God to be missionaries in the fields.

Traditions with respect to roles and structures are simply innovations that hardened. We are all in some way hard-wired for mission, but the movemental impulses are only somewhat preserved in the various institutional structures.

All Christian traditions are indeed part of the larger *one, holy, apostolic, catholic* church at large, and we also have a distinct missional identity among that larger body (1 Cor 12:12-26). We are a particular set of "body parts" among the body, while sharing in the fullness of that greater nature (1 Cor 12:12-26). Almost every new expression is born from a missional impulse, even those that seem forged in the alloy of schism and doctrinal disputes hold to a greater vision of offering Christ to the world.

Bishop Kenneth H. Carter, speaking to the leaders during an annual conference in 2014 said, "The time of the professional minister is over—the time of the missionary pastor has come." That pronouncement set me free, and I have been living into it ever since. At each of the churches I have served, I found a handful of people clinging to life and remembering the "good old days." Essentially, we have planted new churches in the midst of the old ones with the help of a minority of faithful folks. A new creation emerged through the synergistic relationship between those churches. The last thing they needed was a "professional minister" to hold their hand as they died. Instead, they needed "missionary pastors" to journey alongside them as they went out to be the church in the world. Furthermore, this is not the "pastor's job." The loss of the fivefold ministry from Ephesians 4:1-16 (apostle, prophet, evangelist, shepherd, teacher) is in a large part responsible for the massive decline of pastor-centered Christianity in the West.[8]

The term *missionary-pastor* belongs together as a compound word, as demonstrated in the person of Christ who was both "the good shepherd" (John 10:11) and a missionary (Luke 15:4) who came to "seek and save the lost" (Luke 19:10). Jesus is the fullness of the fivefold ministry.

---

8. Hirsch, Catchim, and Breen, *The Permanent Revolution*, 5–9.

He is the totality of what an apostle, prophet, evangelist, shepherd, and teacher can and should be. In Ephesians 4, a letter that circulated to many churches, it takes all of us—collectively—to make one Jesus. Together, the Holy Spirit empowers "God's people for the work of serving and building up the body of Christ until we all reach the unity of faith and knowledge of God's Son. God's goal is for us to become mature adults—to be fully grown, measured by the standard of the fullness of Christ" (Eph 4:12-13).

As Vincent Donovan discovered, the "priesthood" as we know it is an example of culturization originating from the "Graeco-Roman world," not the New Testament. All faithful expressions of the church should be a result of this culturization process (the gospel being planted and growing wild in a context). Yet this requires a contextually appropriate version of a priesthood to grow organically out of those soils. Donavan writes, "Continuing the process with a Western version of the priesthood renders the goal of an adult, indigenous, independent church virtually impossible."[9]

This is what's happening now in fresh expressions, as indigenous leaders in the group rise to become the "priest" of the community. Indeed, this is what each movement did in some way, the cultivation and empowerment of the so-called laity. Indeed, "the world is our parish" and every one of us is sent (ἀπόστολος "apostle" or "sent one") in mission with a part to play.

At Wildwood, after visiting each member in their homes, I literally took my office door off the hinges, placed it in the sanctuary, and preached a series called "Open Door Policy." I lovingly reminded folks I was sent to serve the community as a missionary pastor, not simply the church as personal chaplain.

We regularly hold what we call "body-building gatherings." As the body of Christ, we acknowledge each of us serves specific functions within that body (1 Cor 12:27). We focus on our call as the "apostlehood of believers" (1 Pet 2:4-10). Each of our leaders takes some assessments, including APEST (a profiling instrument designed to help identify your ministry style in relation to the philosophy of the fivefold ministry of

9. Vincent J. Donovan, *Christianity Rediscovered* (Maryknoll, NY: Orbis, 2003), 112.

Ephesians 4[10]), and Gallup's StrengthsFinder. We enter those results into a spreadsheet, and we use team-building resources to understand and develop each other's unique roles. We are also shying away from the catch-all-title of "pastor" for all leaders because it has the baggage of the declining Christendom structures in the West.

The primary tasks of the church, developed around the mission of making disciples, are connected to its very being. Our theological task is to build disciples in a variety of environments and rapidly changing contexts.[11]

While programs and churches don't "make disciples" (the Holy Spirit does), earlier we reviewed how ministries like Celebrate Recovery (a faith application of the 12 Steps), can provide ministry contexts to facilitate the movement of people through the "waves of grace." We use 12 step spirituality as a pathway for the messy relational process of disciple-making.

A typical week in our congregations includes a lay-driven cooperative food pantry that feeds several hundred families, a clothing ministry, interracial unity gatherings, and numerous anonymous and lay-driven recovery fellowships fill the classrooms. We house on our church properties (St Marks and Compassion) residential faith-based rehabilitation centers for women and men called Open Arms Village. Bible studies designed for people at different stages in the journey of grace meet both at the church and in public spaces. Three primary worship experiences gather on Sundays. Prayer gatherings and numerous cooperative outreach ministries, including a large jail ministry, take place as well. Personal and social holiness in the inherited church is still alive!

However, I see discipleship taking place more than anywhere else in our fresh expressions of church. It looks similar to those first incarnational gatherings in fields, barns, homes, theaters, and so on. For us, our fields are Tijuana Flats, dog parks, recreation centers, hair salons, rehabs, assisted living facilities, EV charging stations, tattoo parlors, and VR headsets.

---

10. http://www.theforgottenways.org/apest/.

11. *The Book of Discipline* ¶104, p. 75.

People gather in those spaces, with a desire to enlarge their spiritual lives. John Wesley described the inclusive nature of the small groups in terms of the only requirement for membership was "a desire to flee the wrath to come." This would be considered harmful language today. We don't need to scare the hell out of people into the church, but this was inclusive language for the 1700's and Wesley celebrated this inclusivity as the thing he was most proud of about Methodism.[12] To recode that in today's language, "all our welcome to find healing from the isolation of a hyperconnected world."

In those communities people share honestly about their broken places, illicit affairs, struggles, and loss. A community of love surrounds them as they try to walk with Jesus and grow out of destructive behavior patterns. Many become leaders in their own right, planting their own fresh expression of church, freely giving back the flame of God's love as they have received it. These small communities are indeed salvific, little islands of healing and connection amid a sea of loneliness and isolation. The focus is not on the efforts of singular individuals, but a community that together embodies the mission of God, where each person plays a small role.

Field Story
Theology on Tap
Rev. Isaiah Park
Restoration Church
Reston, Virgina

"It's so easy to invite people to something like this!" This is the spirit of the people participating in Theology on Tap, a Fresh Expression of Restoration Church in Reston, Virginia. Every third Tuesday, people gather at Lake Anne Brew House.

The Lake Anne Brew House tagline is, "Brewing beer and building community." The owners of the brew house are persons of peace who

---

12.   Warner, Laceye, *Knowing Who We Are*, Abingdon Press, 2024, 28.

reached out to Restoration to start Theology on Tap, stating that they have seen Restoration active in the community. In fact, they worked with leaders at Restoration to come up with the name and promote it through their social media channels. They shared, "I won't go to church service, but I'll do Theology on Tap, and we'll support anything that gets the community together."

The venue is bright and has many tables and chairs for people to converse. With joyful anticipation, people arrive to connect and take deep dives into faith. It is an intergenerational experience. The ages of the lay leaders are from young twenties to post-retirement age. Therefore, this Fresh Expression also has age diversity. A new person said, "I can't believe how intergenerational and interactive this gathering is. I'll be back."

No one is ever sitting alone because there is a culture of radical hospitality. As soon as someone walks in, they are greeted and brought into conversation. It is a norm to connect new people to others. One can experience a vibe of openness. When people experience this radical hospitality, they express the desire to serve. A new person shared, "I love this. If you need help with anything, I'm your person. We need more of this."

The Fresh Expression involves prayer, dialogical presentation, conversations, and Q&A. Afterward, people stay to continue connecting with each other. From beginning to end, there is a spirit of excitement, energy, and engagement.

There is a robust sense of invitation and inclusion at Theology on Tap. Restoration has shared that inviting people to Sunday worship is a growing edge, but inviting friends to Theology on Tap is natural. Personal invitation is happening in increasing measure through Fresh Expressions.

Theology on Tap is an open and safe experience. People dive into conversations because the content is accessible. The leadership listens to the input of the people to determine relevant topics. The bartender shared, "I love what you all are doing. You don't have to check your brain at the door when you do church."

Theology on Tap continues to be tethered to the inherited church. The success of Theology on Tap is connected to the inherited church, and the inherited church receives fresh energy and empowerment through Theology on Tap. Furthermore, the success of Theology on Tap has inspired the lay leadership to explore more Fresh Expressions. Through Theology on Tap, Restoration has become a blended ecology that is reaching new people in new ways because "it's so easy to invite people to something like this!"

Missional Field Kit

This is the process for how fresh expressions usually develop:

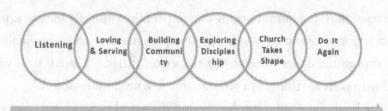

Listening — Loving & Serving — Building Community — Exploring Discipleship — Church Takes Shape — Do It Again

underpinned by prayer, on-going listening, and relationships with the wider church

Stage 1: Listening

The first stage of cultivating fresh expressions involves prayerful listening: to God, the inherited congregation, and the larger community.

Stage 2: Loving and Serving

This is simply about finding ways to be with people in our community, loving and serving them with no agenda.

Stage 3: Building Community

Through the repeated patterns of withness, the loving and serving grows into authentic community. A profound sense of connectedness begins to form, perhaps as we gather around the habitual practices. The relationships have grown beyond whatever hobby, passion, or activity may have initially connected the group.

Stage 4: Exploring Discipleship

Here the group begins to intentionally explore the Christian faith. This occurs through a mixture of both formal learning (intentional conversations) and social learning (simply sharing in the rhythms of life together).

Stage 5: Church Taking Shape

People are beginning to enter and sustain a relationship with Jesus Christ. The marks of the church begin to become a kind of compass for the journey: *one, holy, apostolic, catholic*—in fresh expressions language: *inward, upward, outward,* and *ofward.* (A community unified *in* the faith, growing *up* in worship and holiness, sent *out* in mission to the world, *of* a universal communion of believers throughout all space, time, race, and nation).

Stage 6: Do It Again

Fresh expressions are born pregnant. Once a couple are growing, they begin to multiply. People start to realize, "If so and so can do that . . . I can do this." If Larry can turn his passion for taking his dog to the dog park into church, I can turn my passion for recovering people into church. If church can happen while we run a 5K, it can happen at my workplace. And so on.

1. Where is your team in the process of the fresh expression journey?

2. How might we move to the next stage in the process?

3. Who will be responsible for taking next steps?

God of the Dumpster Dive

The hammock-ridden daughter of an alcoholic with no access to higher education became known as the intellectual and theological brain-child of the Salvation Army. Catherine Mumford was born on January 17, 1829, in Ashbourne, Derbyshire, England, to staunch parents who were active in the temperance movement. Unfortunately, of her four brothers, only John, the youngest, survived infancy. Her mother homeschooled her and despite her limited access to formal education, by twelve she had completed her eighth reading of the entire Bible.[1]

In 1841, when Catherine was twelve, a serious curvature of the spine left her lying facedown in a makeshift hammock for months. This didn't stop her from learning. She began voraciously to study church history and theology. She devoured the writings of John Wesley and John Fletcher. She dove into the works of the Lutheran historians Johann Lorenz Mosheim and Augustus Neander, as well as the American revivalist Charles Finney. She read Joseph Butler's *Analogy of Religion*, Isaac Newton's writings on prophecy, and John Bunyan's *The Pilgrim's Progress*.[2] Her central fascination became the first centuries of Christianity and the teachings and problems of the early church.

---

1. John Read, *Catherine Booth: Laying the Theological Foundations of a Radical Movement* (Eugene, OR: Pickwick, 2013), 6–7.

2. Read, 7

In 1844 her father, once a champion of the temperance movement, relapsed into alcoholism. His business fell into shambles. This along with Catherine's own struggles with the symptoms and side effects of scoliosis, wounded her adolescent years.

On the morning of June 15, 1846, she joyfully shared her conversion with her mother. The familiar words of her hymn book came alive: "My God I am Thine! What a comfort Divine, What a blessing to know that my Jesus is mine!" While this conversion launched her into a soul struggle to pursue sanctification, she lived in constant fear of "backsliding" into sin.[3]

Catherine's longing for the reformation of Methodism was awakened during this time. Shortly after John Wesley's death in 1791, Methodism had begun to splinter into various factions. Many believed the Methodist movement had become domesticated, losing its evangelical fervor and missional focus, existing "as a dead sect, having the form of religion without the power." Various groups represented a movement to reform Methodism. One group broke away as early as 1797 to form the Methodist New Connexion.

Catherine's outspoken support of the reform movement resulted in the nonrenewal of her quarterly Wesleyan Methodist membership ticket. This left her a kind of spiritual orphan for a time. Additionally, throughout the years of 1848–1851, enduring physical pain from both scoliosis and tuberculosis accompanied her spiritual anguish.

None of these adversities, however, were able to stop Catherine Mumford, whom the world would later know as Catherine Booth, cofounder of the Salvation Army.

After her marriage to William Booth on June 16, 1855, Catherine struggled with a stirring that she felt was a call to a public ministry of preaching and teaching. The couple had found a short-lived ministry in the New Methodist Connexion. There she took her first timid steps into her call to public ministry, leading a class meeting, teaching senior girls

---

3.   Read, 7.

Sunday school, and giving temperance lectures. In May 1858 William was ordained as a minister at the New Connexion's annual conference and appointed to Gateshead, where once his requests to evangelistic work were denied, as a superintendent minister.

Walking among the poverty-stricken streets one Sunday evening, Catherine felt a strong compulsion to stop and speak to the women in the dilapidated homes rather than go to the chapel for the service. One woman she encountered was carrying a jug of beer to her alcoholic husband who was bedridden due to his drunken condition. Catherine went to their home, listened intently to their story, then shared the parable of the prodigal son. The encounter left them all in tears. After Catherine led the couple in a time of prayer, she felt a new resolve to begin an evangelistic ministry of visitation, prayer, and practical help.[4]

Catherine was inspired by American holiness revivalist Phoebe Palmer, whose public preaching ministry was bringing hundreds of people to Christ. Phoebe's ministry, however, also attracted powerful critics, who rose up to condemn both revivalism and women's right to preach. This led Catherine, who was yet to speak publicly, to publish her first pamphlet defending the principle of female ministry. Catherine's compelling argument was constructed from a range of Old and New Testament texts. Her essays engaged leading modern and ancient scholars and contained detailed exegeses of scriptural passages that supposedly prohibited female ministry.

Shortly after this, Catherine Booth stepped forward to break her silence and began to speak publicly. She quickly became a celebrity. She spoke to large crowds and was unable to accept the many invitations that poured in. When William became sick, she not only fulfilled his preaching responsibilities but managed the circuit affairs. William ultimately resigned from the Methodist New Connexion, and the Booths became key figures in the Second Evangelical Awakening. Catherine became the prime

---

4. Read, 14

apologist for the movement, not only addressing large crowds, but securing finances, attaining buildings, and organizing the system.

The Booths began evangelizing among those experiencing poverty and oppression in London, England, in 1852. The focus of their ministry was those often neglected or even harmed by the existing churches. They started a movement among the seeming throwaways of church and society. A revival from the fields.

Tragically, Catherine became sick with an aggressive form of breast cancer and deteriorated rapidly. She preached her last sermon on June 21, 1888, at the City Temple in Holborn. She helped prepare the final drafts of *Darkest England,* and floods of faithful visitors came on pilgrimage to visit her sickbed, a kind of altar to her faithfulness to Christ. At her death, the growing army of Salvationists were already scattered across the globe.

She died on Saturday October 4, 1890, and her body was taken to the Army's Clapton Congress Hall. An estimated fifty thousand people came to her lying in state. Thousands more attended her funeral services, and the *Methodist Times* described Catherine as the Army's "inspiring soul" and "restraining genius."[5]

Catherine Booth is the mother of Salvation Army theology. From her mind, heart, and soul, the movement of Salvationism was unleashed on the world. It is a movement that has touched millions of lives, brought ministry to the darkest places, and encouraged the acceptance of women in ministry. Today, the Salvation Army reports a worldwide membership of over 1.7 million, consisting of soldiers, officers, and adherents who are collectively known as salvationists. Salvation Army places of worship are sometimes called 'citadels' or 'temples,' but they are often located among the underserved and economically vulnerable. Many Salvation Army centers also serve as emergency housing facilities, transitional living centers, group homes, and family shelters. Salvationists provide more than 8 million nights of lodging annually.

5. Read, 25.

They also help provide financial assistance to cover emergency overnight housing costs or refer those facing housing and food insecurity to trusted partner programs with emergency shelter services. In addition to supplying beds, food, shelter from the elements, and basic hygiene resources to those in need, Salvation Army sites help combat long-term homelessness by providing homeless adults, veterans, and children with holistic physical, emotional, and spiritual support. In addition to providing food and lodging, their centers offer educational support, counseling, and vocational services to houseless individuals, families, and vulnerable youth. They provide dedicated on-site caseworkers to help clients embrace responsibility, meet important goals, and gain self-sufficiency.

For the early Salvationists, God was present in the "dumpster dive." A seeking and sending God of relentless love visits dumpsters to recover what others have thrown away, including the people who are societies' throwaways. God, like a good shepherd, leaves the ninety-nine to go after the one (Luke 15:4). This is a God who gets down on her hands and knees until she finds a lost coin (Luke 15:8). God is like a father who runs towards a prodigal son while he is still "a far way off" (Luke 15:20). The God of resurrection takes what's decaying, broken, dead, and makes it "new creation." Not one day, by and by, but right now.

To be in a relationship with God, to love one's neighbor, this is the taste of heaven. It was a pervasive belief among those first Salvationists that the new creation is unfolding now. Love awakened the Booth's hearts. Love sent them to the slums among the poor and marginalized. Perfect love of God and neighbor in this life by faith is a foretaste of God's kingdom come on the earth. The risen spirit of Jesus is available to be breathed in and received. God's kingdom is at hand and eternal life starts now. This is the blazing hope that shined in *Darkest England*.

The Salvation message wasn't simply accepting Jesus now "to go to heaven when we die." The way to heaven was a journey that started in this life. It was this urgency and invitation that stirred folks to respond. It was this understanding that drove them into the pain, to pursue this kingdom life now, and it still drives Salvationists today.

Time for a Remix

In a consumeristic culture of the network society, where everything is commoditized, individualized, and disposable, the dumpsters are full. A culture of consumerism creates a culture of waste. We throw away the outdated for the next new upgrade. We are caught up in a never-ending pursuit of the next newfangled thing. Unfortunately, not only do things become disposable in our system, but so do people. People who get in the way. People who don't contribute to our culture of sharing, remixing, and innovating.

In a culture obsessed with all new things, God makes all things new (Rev 21:5). God's way is not about discarding the old for the next new upgrade. God refuses to scrap the project in a dumpster and start over. God is a God of the remix, refreshing the existing material, reshaping and recoding. God's way of "making all things new" is about resurrection. It's about empty tombs, marred clay reworked in the potter's hands, and healed lives. Resurrection is a power that breaks death, reverses the process of decay, recycles refuse, and makes churches come back to life. God is making the cosmos new in this way, right now (Rom 8:19-23).

I was involved in a substance-abuse intervention that resulted in a very public, miraculous healing. I was contacted by a family to lead a last-chance intervention for their son Jeff. The kingdom of God showed up in an apartment that smelled like feces and booze that morning, when he said, "Yes" to some help. After taking him to the facility the family had in place, he was immediately transferred to the hospital, where he was given two months to live and sent to hospice.

His parents requested our team to pray over him. Within days he had an incredible turn around, was released from hospice, and entered a recovery program. Dubbed a modern day "Lazarus" because of the very dramatic nature of Jeff's healing, his story created a buzz on several front-page features.[6] Jeff became a leader at our church, which has become a station of hope for those struggling with addiction, and furthermore a sign and foretaste of God's kingdom.

"With other Christians we recognize that the reign of God is both a present and future reality. The church is called to be that place where the first signs of the reign of God are identified and acknowledged in the world. . . . We also look to the end time in which God's work will be fulfilled."[7] Jesus's preaching on God's kingdom, inextricably linked to his identity, was not about a "postmortem destiny" or an escape hatch from some evil universe but about "God's sovereign rule" showing up on this earth, here and now, as it is in heaven.[8]

While Jeff is an extreme example, he is a living illustration of a Christian understanding of how God's reign is spreading through creation. For some people, Jeff's nickname and subsequent ministry, the "Lazarus Walk" (John 11), illustrates God's incredible power to resuscitate those who are dead. Jeff's healing is a powerful example of someone who has entered into the eternal life now and has become a citizen of God's inbreaking realm. Jeff ultimately died years later as a sober Christian; after he surrendered to Jesus in that hospice bed, his life was transformed. He authored several Christian children's books. He made an impact in the lives of his family and community. He died anticipating with bold faith the resurrection life to come.

Displacing our hope for eternal life to some distant celestial shore, disembodied from our current physical state, is the same misconception Martha has in the Lazarus story when she says, "Lord, I know one day. . . ." But Jesus confronts her misunderstanding with a powerful truth: "I am

---

6. If you are interested in learning more about Jeff's incredible healing and subsequent ministry, see: http://www.villages-news.com/thankful-for-a-second-chance-man-embarks-on-daily-lazarus-walk/.

7. *The Book of Discipline*, ¶101, p. 44.

8. N. T. Wright, *Surprised by Hope: Rethinking Heaven, the Resurrection, and the Mission of the Church* (New York: HarperOne, 2008), 18.

the resurrection and the life; those who believe in me will never die" (John 11:21-27). Jesus comes to give us an eternal life now and share in unending relationship with God.

I have witnessed many stories like Jeff's: people who once seemed broken beyond repair are made new. When the lives of the lost and broken, rich and miserable, and incarcerated or addicted enter the Kingdom, die to self, and live for Christ, they are transformed into new creatures. They begin living presently in the newness of eternal life, giving themselves as the ingredients of God's cosmic renewal that will soon be fully realized.

This expectation is a regular activity in fresh expressions of church. "Dones," people who feel like the church's throw aways, are finding a relationship with God again. "Nones," people with slight awareness that something is missing in their lives, are finding meaning, purpose, and taking their place in God's great recovery effort. People who only saw a mess when they looked in the mirror, isolated in their shame, are hearing the Spirit whisper "masterpiece," "beloved," and "very good." People who will never walk into our Sunday morning church services are finding new life in Christ in the fields of their everyday lives. They are becoming "new creation" and becoming the ingredients of the cosmic work of renewal that God is up to.

A waste-saturated culture throws away the obsolete for the next new upgrade. Even people become disposable commodities, especially Brown immigrants at our borders, or Black prisoners whose unjust incarceration has been monetized in for-profit prison systems, or our religious and political others, elderly saints who have lived beyond their "usefulness" and are now euthanized or warehoused in care facilities. Yet amid this great crisis of our age—the devaluing of human lives in a consumerist culture of extraction, commoditization, and violence—God is making the dumpster dive, and fresh expressions of church are God's hands and feet.

This is my hope for all Christians. Although it seems the world has disposed of denominations in the ecclesial dumpster, God is calling us to join along in the dumpster-diving activities. Fresh Expressions is one of the powerful ways God is recovering lives that have been thrown away. The denominational impulse of our various faith traditions is often self-preservation (the first sin instinct, Genesis 3), but the way of Jesus is self-donation (Philippians 2). Self-donation is ritualized as the centerpiece of worship in the Lord's Supper, the body is taken, blessed, broken, and given. "Make them be for us the body and blood of Jesus—so that we may be the body and blood of Jesus in the world." We too are taken, blessed, broken, and given. This movement from the fields enables us to recover an ecclesiology of gift. The Eucharistic nature of the body of Christ is to be broken and given to a hungry world.

This is the way forward to true revitalization: dying and giving ourselves away in this effort. Dying is actually a movement in the process of resurrection; a seed that never goes into the ground never produces fruit (John 12:24). As Jim Harnish says regarding church revitalization, *You Only Have to Die*.[9] Cultivating fresh expressions allows us to give ourselves away to our communities. It's allowing us to plant seeds of the gospel that will grow wild as an indigenous expression of the church in a post-Christendom network society. I hope this field guide will help you to join into the activity of a dumpster diving God. A God of resurrection.

Field Story
Compassion
Rev. Jill Beck
United Methodist Church
Ocala, Florida

Are there lessons from the Fresh Expressions way that can be applied to more "conventional" church planting? Let me tell you the story of Compassion UMC.

My husband and I are co-pastors in North Central Florida. We have been pastoring churches and cultivating fresh expressions across the area

---

9. James A. Harnish, *You Only Have to Die: Leading Your Congregation to New Life* (Nashville: Abingdon Press, 2004), 11.

for sixteen years. At St. Marks in Ocala, we have multiple fresh expressions meeting each week, tethered to the existing congregation. On average we see about 300 people gathering in this ecology of church weekly. We are also home to a holistic recovery housing program for men called Open Arms Village (OAV).

We were truly excited when a new opportunity opened on the opposite side of the city. A church had closed there and was sitting vacant for several years. We would often see people experiencing homelessness camping out at various spots around the campus. Sometimes I would stop and see if I could help them. I often prayed over the campus. The Holy Spirit was stirring something in my soul.

I shared a vision with our district and conference leadership. My proposal was to start with the deepest needs in our community and see if a new faith community might spring up out of a coalition of people seeking to meet those needs together.

In Fresh Expressions we follow the "loving first journey." We listen, love and serve, build relationships, and explore discipleship; church takes shape, and then we multiply. We held a community listening session at the vacant site, inviting people in the neighborhood to come out and share what the greatest needs and opportunities were. Food insecurity, homelessness, substance abuse, and a rise in overdose deaths were some of the big challenges. A lack of recovery housing for women was at the top of the list.

As a woman who was once a resident in a domestic violence shelter, I've always had a passion to help other women in adverse circumstances. In collaboration with our OAV board, we decided we would convert the vacant church facility into a women's recovery housing program. The site would also be home to a new faith community, Compassion UMC. We assembled a team for a Tuesday night community dinner, alongside a Sunday morning worship experience. We utilized our connections to move several large recovery groups into the space, and the campus is now busy seven days a week. From the beginning we have sought to be a blended ecology.

At our opening worship and block party, we had three circuit court judges, a seminary president, two construction business owners, a bank president, the director of the local rehab, the Ocala mayor, and people celebrating days and months of clean time from intravenous drug use, all worshiping together. In other words, the kingdom!

Now my friends experiencing homelessness come inside for dinner every Tuesday, to rest, eat, and charge their phones. The chemical dependency unit director buses over the female residents every week. Our board raised $150,000 dollars in the first week toward the renovation.

Each day a place that once was vacant is now a place of life and healing for the marginalized in our community. The Fresh Expressions way might just have something to teach the whole church about starting with the compassion of Jesus and seeing what might emerge.

Missional Field Kit: Recoding Exercise

With your team, consider together whether the people in your community are hearing your message as "good news."

If we want emerging generations to hear God's news as good news, we should start where God starts. . . "very good."

We need to also share the good news not only where it is "good" but where it also "news." How would you share the gospel with someone who has never heard it before? In a culture that communicates in tweets, how might you share the gospel in a concise but impactful way?

Here's a fun field kit exercise for your team to do together:

What Is the Good News?

Write a definition of the gospel in

> 144 characters (Have each person on the team try to share the gospel in a "tweet.")

1 sentence (Have each person try to share the gospel in one
sentence.)

3 words (Now try to share the gospel in three words!)

Reflect on your responses together.

A Mature Fresh Expression

How can your team know the difference between a "potential" and
"mature" fresh expression? Or what indicators can we use to distinguish
between, say, an outreach and a new church? I have developed the "Four
C's" as a kind of guide to help:

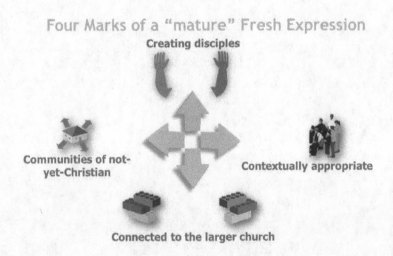

Four Marks of a "mature" Fresh Expression

Creating disciples

Communities of not-yet-Christian

Contextually appropriate

Connected to the larger church

Cultivating disciples: Disciples of Jesus Christ are being formed.
This is not just playing church.

Communities of non-Christians: These are gatherings with and for
people who are not Christian. They are not just groups of already-
Christians hanging out in the community.

Contextually appropriate: This community has emerged organically from the context; it takes on the shape, patterns, and language of the people there. This is not planting our colonial "version of church" in foreign soils.

Connected to the larger church: The fresh expression is tethered to the inherited church in some relational way. These are not little colonies isolated from or in opposition to the inherited church.

With your team, talk through the Four C's. Do you see each one in the fresh expression(s) you are pioneering? If not, what could you do to grow in that area?

Credits

Arbuckle, Gerald A. *Refounding the Church: Dissent for Leadership*. Maryknoll, NY: Orbis, 1993.

Avis, Paul D. *The Oxford Handbook of Ecclesiology*. Oxford: Oxford University Press, 2018.

Backert, Chris. "Emerging Church and Missional Church: Same Difference?" *Fresh Expressions US*. April 18, 2016. http://freshexpressionsus.org/2016/04/18/emerging-church-missional-church-difference/.

Backert, Chris. https://freshexpressionsus.org/2018/12/10/fresh-expressions-us-year-end-review-2018/

Baker, John. *Celebrate Recovery*. Grand Rapids, MI: Zondervan, 2012.

Baker, Jonny, and Cathy Ross. *The Pioneer Gift: Explorations in Mission*. Norwich, UK: Canterbury Press, 2014.

Beck, Michael. *Deep Roots, Wild Branches: Revitalizing the Church in the Blended Ecology*. Franklin, TN: Seedbed Publishing, 2019.

Beck, Michael. http://freshexpressionsus.org/2017/09/06/fresh-approach-charlottesville/

Beck, Michael. https://freshexpressionsus.org/2018/03/05/history-repeating-discipleship/

Bettenson, Henry S., and Chris Maunder. *Documents of the Christian Church*. Oxford and New York: Oxford University Press, 1999.

Bevans, Stephen B. and Roger P. Schroeder. *Constants in Context*. Maryknoll, NY: Orbis, 2004.

Bevans, Stephen B. and Roger Schroeder. *Prophetic Dialogue: Reflections on Christian Mission Today*. Maryknoll, NY: Orbis, 2011.

Bolger, Ryan K. 2007. "Practice Movements in Global Information Culture: Looking Back to McGavran and Finding a Way Forward." *Missiology* 35, no. 2: 181–93, http://journals.sagepub.com.georgefox.idm.oclc.org/doi/pdf/10.1177/009182960703500208.

Bonhoeffer, Dietrich. *Life Together*. New York: Harper and Row, 1954.

Bonhoeffer, Dietrich. *The Cost of Discipleship*. New York: Touchstone, 1995.

Bosch, David J. *Transforming Mission: Paradigm Shifts in Theology of Mission*. Maryknoll, NY: Orbis, 1991.

Bolton, Bill, and John Thompson. *Entrepreneurs: Talent, Temperament and Opportunity*. London, UK, and New York: Routledge, 2013.

Brafman, Ori, and Rod A. Beckstrom. *The Starfish and the Spider: The Unstoppable Power of Leaderless Organizations*. New York: Portfolio, 2014.

Brueggemann, Walter. *Finally Comes the Poet*. Minneapolis: Fortress, 1989.

Butcher, James N., Susan Mineka, and Jill Hooley. *Abnormal Psychology: Core Concepts*. Allyn and Bacon: Boston, 2008.

Carter, Ken. "Church Vitality" https://www.flumc.org/church-vitality

Castells, Manuel. *The Rise of the Network Society*. Oxford and Malden, MA: Blackwell Publishers, 2000.

Chilcote, Paul W. *Active Faith: Resisting 4 Dangerous Ideologies with the Wesleyan Way*. Nashville: Abingdon Press, 2019.

Chilcote, Paul W. *John and Charles Wesley: Selections from Their Writings and Hymns*. Woodstock, VT: SkyLight Paths Publications, 2011.

Chilcote, Paul W. *Recapturing the Wesleys' Vision: An Introduction to the Faith of John and Charles Wesley*. Downers Grove, IL: InterVarsity Press, 2004.

Chilcote, Paul W. *The Wesleyan Tradition: A Paradigm for Renewal*. Nashville: Abingdon Press, 2002.

Clayton, M. Christensen, Michael E. Raynor, and Rory McDonald. "What Is Disruptive Innovation?" *Harvard Business Review*. December 2015. Accessed October 20, 2017. https://hbr.org/2015/12/what-is-disruptive-innovation.

Collins, Kenneth J. *The Theology of John Wesley: Holy Love and the Shape of Grace*. Nashville: Abingdon Press, 2007.

Collins, Travis. *From the Steeple to the Street: Innovating Mission and Ministry Through Fresh Expressions of Church*. Franklin, TN: Seedbed Publishing, 2016.

Cooper, Burton. *Why, God?* Atlanta: John Knox Press, 1988.

Cray, Graham. *Mission-Shaped Church: Church Planting and Fresh Expressions in a Changing Context*. New York: Seabury Books, 2010.

Cray, Graham, Ian Mobsby, and Aaron Kennedy. *Fresh Expressions of Church and the Kingdom of God*. Norwich, UK: Canterbury Press, 2012.

Croft, Steven J. *The Future of the Parish System: Shaping the Church of England for the Twenty-First Century*. London, UK: Church House, 2006.

D'Ambrosio, Marcellino. *When the Church Was Young: Voices of the Early Fathers*. Cincinnati, OH: Servant Books, 2014.

Danker, Ryan N. *Wesley and the Anglicans: Political Division in Early Evangelicalism*. Downers Grove, IL: IVP Academic, an imprint of InterVarsity Press, 2016.

Donovan, Vincent J. *Christianity Rediscovered*. Maryknoll, N.Y.: Orbis, 2003.

Enns, Peter. *Inspiration and Incarnation: Evangelicals and the Problem of the Old Testament*. Grand Rapids, MI: Baker Academic, 2005.

Felton, Gayle C. *United Methodists and the Sacraments*. Nashville: Abingdon Press, 2007.

Frost, Michael, and Alan Hirsch. *ReJesus: A Wild Messiah for a Missional Church*. Peabody, MA, and Sydney: Hendrickson Publishers, Strand Pub, 2009.

Fujimura, Makoto. *Culture Care: Reconnecting with Beauty for Our Common Life*. New York: Fujimura Institute, 2014.

González, Justo L. *A History of Christian Thought. Vol. 1: From the Beginnings to the Council of Chalcedon*. Rev. ed., 22. print. Vol. 1. Nashville: Abingdon Press, 1996.

González, Justo L. *The Story of Christianity. Volume 1: The Early Church to the Reformation*. Rev. and Updated [ed.], 2nd ed. New York: HarperCollins, 2010.

González, Justo L. *The Story of Christianity. Volume 2: The Reformation to the Present Day*. Rev. and Updated [ed.], 2nd ed. New York: HarperCollins, 2010.

Goodhew, David, Andrew Roberts, and Michael Volland. *Fresh!: An Introduction to Fresh Expressions of Church and Pioneer Ministry*. London, UK: SCM Press, 2012.

Guthrie, Shirley C. *Christian Doctrine*. Louisville, KY: Westminster John Knox, 1994.

Hamilton, Adam. *Making Sense of the Bible: Rediscovering the Power of Scripture Today*. New York: HarperOne, 2014.

Harnish, James A. *You Only Have to Die: Leading Your Congregation to New Life*. Nashville: Abingdon Press, 2004.

Harper, Steve. *Devotional Life in the Wesleyan Tradition*. Nashville: Upper Room Books, 1995.

Harper, S. *The Way to Heaven: The Gospel According to John Wesley*. Grand Rapids, MI: Zondervan, 2003.

Haynes, Donald. *On the Threshold of Grace: Methodist Fundamentals*. Dallas: UMR Communications, 2010.

Heath, Elaine A., and Larry Duggins. *Missional, Monastic, Mainline: A Guide to Starting Missional Micro-Communities in Historically Mainline Traditions*. Eugene, OR: Cascade, 2014

Heim, S. Mark. *Saved From Sacrifice: A Theology of the Cross*. Grand Rapids, MI: Eerdmans, 2006.

Heitzenrater, Richard P. *Wesley and the People Called Methodists*. Nashville: Abingdon Press, 1995.

Hirsch, Alan, and Dave Ferguson. *On the Verge: A Journey into the Apostolic Future of the Church*. Grand Rapids, MI: Zondervan, 2011.

Hirsch, Alan, Tim Catchim, and Mike Breen. *The Permanent Revolution: Apostolic Imagination and Practice for the 21st Century Church*. San Francisco: Jossey-Bass, 2012.

Hirsch, Alan. *The Forgotten Ways: Reactivating the Missional Church*. Grand Rapids, MI: Brazos, 2006.

Hirsch, Alan. *5Q: Reactivating the Original Intelligence and Capacity of the Body of Christ*. USA: 100M, 2017.

Hodgett, T., and P. Bradbury. "Pioneering Mission is…a spectrum." ANVIL 34, no. 1. Accessed January 5, 2019. https://churchmissionsociety.org/resources/pioneering-mission-spectrum-tina-hodgett-paul-bradbury-anvil-vol-34-issue-1/

Inbody, Tyron. *The Faith of the Christian Church: An Introduction to Theology* (Grand Rapids, MI: Eerdmans, 2005), 155–57.

Jones, Angela. *Pioneer Ministry and Fresh Expressions of Church*. London, UK: SPCK, 2009.

Jones, Scott J. *United Methodist Doctrine: The Extreme Center*. Nashville: Abingdon Press, 2002.

Küng, Hans. *The Church*. Garden City, NY: Image Books, 1976.

Laytham, D. B. *God Does Not Entertain, Play "Matchmaker," Hurry, Demand Blood, Cure Every Illness*. Grand Rapids, MI: Brazos Press, 2009.

Long, Thomas G. *What Shall We Say?: Evil, Suffering, and the Crisis of Faith*. Grand Rapids, MI: Eerdmans, 2011.

Maddox, R. and Runyon, T. *Rethinking Wesley's Theology for Contemporary Methodism*. Nashville: Kingswood, 1998.

Maddox, R. *Responsible Grace: John Wesley's Practical Theology*. Nashville: Kingswood, 1994.

Male, David. *Pioneers 4 Life: Explorations in Theology and Wisdom for Pioneering Leaders*. Abingdon: Bible Reading Fellowship, 2011.

Male, David. "Do We Need Pioneers?" 2017. https://freshexpressions.org.uk/get-started/pioneer-ministry/.

McGavran, Donald A. *The Bridges of God: A Study in the Strategy of Missions*. Eugene, Ore: Wipf & Stock, 2005.

McGrath, Alister E. *Christian Theology: An Introduction*. Chichester, West Sussex, United Kingdom and Malden, MA: Wiley-Blackwell, 2011.

Migliore, Daniel L. *Faith Seeking Understanding: An Introduction to Christian Theology*. Grand Rapids, MI: Eerdmans, 2014.

Moltmann, Jürgen. *The Church in the Power of the Spirit: A Contribution to Messianic Ecclesiology*. Minneapolis: Fortress, 1993.

Moltmann, Jürgen *The Crucified God: The Cross of Christ as the Foundation and Criticism of Christian Theology*. Minneapolis: Fortress, 1993.

Moynagh, Michael. *Being Church, Doing Life: Creating Gospel Communities Where Life Happens*. Oxford, England, UK and Grand Rapids, MI: Monarch, 2014.

Moynagh, Michael, and Philip Harrold. *Church for Every Context: An Introduction to Theology and Practice*. London, UK: SCM Press, 2012.

Moynagh, Michael. *Church in Life: Emergence, Ecclesiology and Entrepreneurship*. London, UK: SCM Press, 2017.

Moynagh, Michael, and Richard Worsley. *Going Global: Key Questions for the Twenty-First Century*. London, UK: A and C Black, 2008.

Murray, Ian. *Wesley and the Men Who Followed.* Edinburgh: The Banner of Truth Trust, 2003.

Murray, Stuart. *Church After Christendom.* Milton Keynes: Paternoster Press, 2004.

Nelstrop, Louise, and Martyn Percy. *Evaluating Fresh Expressions: Explorations in Emerging Church: Responses to the Changing Face of Ecclesiology in the Church of England.* Norwich: Canterbury Press, 2008.

Newbigin, Lesslie. *Foolishness to the Greeks: The Gospel and Western Culture.* Grand Rapids, MI: Eerdmans, 1986.

Newbigin, Lesslie. *The Good Shepherd: Meditations on Christian Ministry in Today's World.* Grand Rapids, MI: Eerdmans, 1977.

Oldenburg, Ray. *The Great Good Place: Cafés, Coffee Shops, Bookstores, Bars, Hair Salons, and Other Hangouts at the Heart of a Community.* New York and Berkeley, CA: Marlowe, Distributed by Publishers Group West, 1999.

Peterson, Eugene. *Eat This Book: A Conversation in the Art of Spiritual Reading.* Grand Rapids, MI: Eerdmans, 2006.

Rendle, Gilbert R. *Quietly Courageous: Leading the Church in a Changing World.* Lanham, MD: Rowman and Littlefield, 2019.

Roxburgh, Alan J. *Structured for Mission: Renewing the Culture of the Church.* Downers Grove, IL: InterVarsity, 2015.

Runyon, Theodore. *The New Creation: John Wesley's Theology Today.* Nashville: Abingdon, 1998.

Russell, Brian. *Realigning with God: Reading Scripture for Church and World.* Eugene, OR: Cascade, 2015.

Sarasvathy, Saras D., "What Makes Entrepreneurs Entrepreneurial?" https://dx.doi.org/

Smith, Heather. "Inside America's Largest Religious Revival You Know Nothing About" *The Federalist.* November 2017. http://thefederalist.com/2017/11/10/inside-americas-largest-religious-revival-know-nothing/ Accessed November 2017.

Sweet, Leonard I. *The Greatest Story Never Told: Revive Us Again.* Nashville: Abingdon Press, 2012.

Sweet, Leonard I. *Me and We: God's New Social Gospel*. Nashville: Abingdon Press, 2014.

Sykes, Stephen, John E. Booty, and Jonathan Knight. *The Study of Anglicanism*. London, UK: SPCK/Fortress, 1998.

Tamez, Elsa. *The Amnesty of Grace: Justification by Faith from a Latin American Perspective*. Nashville: Abingdon Press, 1993.

Taylor, Paul. *The Next America: Boomers, Millennials, and the Looming Generational Showdown*. New York: Public Affairs, 2015.

The United Methodist Hymnal. Nashville: The United Methodist Publishing House, 1989.

Vocations to Pioneer Ministry. https://www.cofepioneer.org/assessment/

Weems, Lovett H. *Focus: The Real Challenges That Face The United Methodist Church*. Nashville: Abingdon Press, 2011.

Wesley, John, et al. *The Works of John Wesley*. Nashville: Abingdon Press, 1984.

Wesley, John. *The Works of John Wesley*. Peabody, MA: Hendrickson Publishers, 1984.

Wesley, John, and Albert C. Outler. *John Wesley*. New York: Oxford University Press, 1964.

Willimon, William H. *This We Believe: The Core of Wesleyan Faith and Practice*. Nashville: Abingdon Press, 2010.

Willimon, William H. *United Methodist Beliefs: A Brief Introduction*. Louisville, KY: Westminster John Knox, 2007.

Willimon, William H. *Who Will Be Saved?* Nashville: Abingdon Press, 2008.

Willimon, William H. *Why I Am a United Methodist*. Nashville: Abingdon Press, 1990.

Wood, Arthur S. *The Burning Heart: John Wesley, Evangelist*. Minneapolis: Bethany Fellowship, 1978.

Wright, Christopher J. H. *The Mission of God: Unlocking the Bible's Grand Narrative*. Downers Grove, IL: InterVarsity, 2006.

Wright, N. T. *Surprised by Hope: Rethinking Heaven, the Resurrection, and the Mission of the Church*. New York: HarperOne, 2008.

Alternate Ending

On a landscape of decline, can our church experience an alternate ending?

I am one of those people who is consistently the last one to leave the movie theater. I always wait for all the credits to roll. Sometimes the movie was so touching that I need a couple of minutes to process it and identify places where I saw the Gospel. Sometimes there is a little trailer to a sequel, a final hidden scene, or an alternate ending. You have made it all the way to the credits of this story. After all is said and done, this is the question I want you to leave with: Can my church experience an alternate ending?

I know the frustration of giving your life for a church, giving your prime years, giving all you have, yet it continues to decline. I know about the sleepless nights, the neglected families, the constant state of fatigue. If you know those feelings, this book was really written for you. I wrote it because I honestly believe fresh expressions is the greatest hope for reaching people, transforming communities, and potentially revitalizing a congregation.

I have seen it work, and I have seen it fail. But God has recently brought to my awareness that what we consider failure on this side of eternity looks different from God's perspective.

I want to leave you with a final image to illustrate what I mean. An incredible book on polycentric leadership is Brafman and Beckstrom's

The Starfish and the Spider: The Unstoppable Power of Leaderless Organizations.[1] They offer examples of both centralized and decentralized leadership, analyzing them closely with a hybrid organization that very much resembles the blended ecology way. One of the most powerful lessons in the book was this: starfish and spiders may appear structurally similar, but there is a major distinction. When you cut the head off of a spider—it dies. However, when you cut a starfish in half, it replicates, becoming two starfish.

Some inherited congregations will die, no matter what we do. Unfortunately, it is usually the people in those congregations that will inadvertently cause their death. If they are not willing to die to self and open themselves to the resurrection power of the God who is making all things new, they may close. However, the blended ecology way leaves a new kind of church in the communities where the inherited congregation once was—a network of churches in the flows, which may become the future church of that community.

I don't know what will happen to the denomination I have given my life to serve. Yet, at the end of the day, measuring not the numbers but the stories, I have seen God retrieve so many once fragmented souls, heal them, and send them to change the world. That is the real legacy that we leave behind—transformed lives. Whether the brick and mortar realities endure or not, the people that we share life with in these fresh expressions will continue to be the church where the church is not. Those that have heard the call and responded will be the cultivators who plant the seeds of what the church will be. Give your energy to creating starfish, not spiders. Plant the seeds of trees you may never see grow.

The final scene of our story is a diverse and unified humanity, gathered together again at the tree of life. The leaves of the tree are for the healing of the nations, and God will wipe away every tear from our eyes

---

1. Ori, Brafman and Rod A. Beckstrom, *The Starfish and the Spider: The Unstoppable Power of Leaderless Organizations* (New York: Portfolio, 2014).

(Rev 21–22). Let's cultivate communities that look like that coming urban garden of new creation . . . now. It is my deepest prayer for you that your churches and communities will experience an alternative ending. One of death and resurrection, but not closure.

See you at the tree, my friends!